Men are from Earth
Women are from Earth

DEAL WiTH it

Men are from Earth
Women are from Earth

DEAL WiTH it

GSOH

First published in the United Kingdom in 2005 by Little Books Ltd,
48 Catherine Place, London SW1E 6HL

10 9 8 7 6 5 4 3 2 1

A CIP catalogue record for this book is available from the British Library.

ISBN: 1 904435 32 7

Many thanks to: Jamie Ambrose for editorial production and management,
Debbie Clement for jacket design,
Mousemat Design Limited for production consulting and text design,
and Claudia Dowell for proofreading.

Printed and bound in Great Britain by William Clowes Ltd, Beccles, Suffolk

Contents

God Is Dead and the Plumber Can't Come on Tuesday 8

Communication
Why no one listens anymore   16

Ego
Ego is to planet as genitalia is to atom   26

Alphas
Power games have leather accessories   34

Body Image
How to turn a frog into a toad   44

Flirting
Simply connect. Alternatively, screw the whole thing up 55

Dating
It's not for life, it's only an evening, for God's sake 64

Speed Dating
Love always speaks its name and email   74

Unrequited Love
Men have died... but not for love   85

Sex
  The birds and bees can keep it   95

Food
  There's no such thing as a little bit of garlic   106

Parties
  I should have stayed at home   117

Bad Behaviour
  Chivalry isn't dead, it's in a permanent vegetative state   130

Work
  All play and no work makes for big trouble   138

Holidays
  Get away from it all. Alternatively, take it all with you   148

Commitment
  Those who want to commit often should be   157

Moving In
  Love & surrender (your possessions, your sanity, your remote...)166

Bad Habits
  From Brad Pitt to Arm Pit   178

War Zones
  I told you not to go down there   188

Money
Liquid assets have a way of leaking   201

Friends
A friend in need is a bleeding pain   211

Infidelity
Sex now, pay later   224

Rows
Arguments clear the ornaments   232

Apologies
Love means always having to say you're sorry   244

Breaking Up
They said it wouldn't work – and they were right   253

Exes
Feel the fear and forget it   264

Living Together
Home is where you go when the pub shuts   274

Family
God sends you friends, the Inquisition sends you relations 283

Babies
Something to do when there's nothing on telly   295

God Is Dead, and the Plumber Can't Come on Tuesday

Once upon a time being a woman was simple. All you had to do was be nice, look nice, talk nice, cook nice and you'd be kept for life. Being a man was just as simple. You had to be hard: work hard, play hard, display no emotion unless in the total darkness of the marital bedroom, and you would reap the rewards of being a 'proper man'. There was no room for either sex to rebel unless they were brave enough to accept ostracism. For those of both sexes who lacked the courage to rebel, it could mean a life of quiet misery.

Now all things are becoming possible. Women can be assertive, men can cry or push a pram without someone calling the thought police. A wonderful world of individuality and cooperation beckons, but while we flounder on the edge of this revolution, no one seems certain of which way to go to be themselves.

In other words, it's a FUBAR*.

Scientists claim there are definite differences between the sexes; feminists scream victimization; men whinge that women threaten to take over the world. No

* FUBAR: Fucked Up Beyond All Recognition

8

one, it seems, is happy, so just who IS in the driving seat? Not men, if adverts are anything to go by.

No wonder the poor little darlings feel threatened. A lager commercial shows a wife forcing her husband to clean lager off the floor with his tongue. A jeans poster shows a man naked under a woman's stiletto heel accompanied by the slogan 'Put the boot in'. A bread advert shows a wife banishing a man to the shed in front of his children as punishment for not eating his sandwich. A television programme advocates moulding your man using dog-training techniques. Yes, collars and leads aren't just for the bedroom anymore!

And yet, while women appear to crack the whip, their average take-home pay is less than three-quarters that of men. Only eighteen percent of MPs are female, and all the great offices of state are held by men.

Parity, let alone domination, is still a long way off.

Yet do women merit equality? Recent research claims that men have a significantly superior intelligence to women – a difference of five IQ points. If this were true, it would mean men should do better than women in a wide variety of intellectual challenges. That's impressive but did the researchers take account of Man's freedom to concentrate on the task in hand while Woman multi-tasks: holding down jobs, rearing children, running homes, coping with ageing relatives (his and hers) and reminding him he's due at the dentist? The fact that women can do three things at once is a source of annoyance to men, but that doesn't stop them expecting her to massage their ego with one hand, sugar their tea with the other and rock the cradle with her foot.

The thesis is further blown apart by statistics which show that young women are obtaining more and better A-levels than young men. Where are the IQ points there? There is also evidence from more than twenty countries to suggest that men have been conditioned to overestimate their IQs and women to doubt theirs. Perhaps we tend to be as smart as we have been led to believe we are – or as dumb.

If today's men are over-estimating their IQs, however, they are increasingly dubious about everything else. They doubt their ability to make a relationship or, once made, to hold it together. Once upon a time it was women who faked orgasm; according to an internet survey, now fifteen percent of men admit to it – and almost half that admit to faking most of the time. In addition, family doctors in Britain revealed that as many as 2.5 million men could be suffering from infertility, brought on in part by stress, although smoking and alcohol were the chief culprits.

As if that weren't enough, a broadsheet survey found that women are more than eight times more likely to cite boredom with their partner as reason for divorce. And hen nights and Ann Summers parties not only flourish, they are said to be more valued than sex with a partner.

Coming second to the Rampant Rabbit cannot be good for male morale, so it's not surprising that men have become increasingly narcissistic. Their magazines publish coquettish pictures of semi-naked heroes, Beckham being prominent among them. Shaved, moisturized, styled by an expert, they bear as much relation to the masculine figure of the Forties and Fifties as Woody Allen does to Schwarzenegger.

Today's man strains to suggest bisexuality. He has become his own love object – not so much in touch with his feminine side as engulfed by it. Male spending on gym membership, grooming products and cosmetic surgery has rocketed. Magazines are predicting the eventual emergence of the *über*sexual male, a man who will revert to simple showering and downing pints instead of Pinot Grigio – but I wouldn't bet on men giving up their new-found crutches: the creams and potions once sacred to women.

Meanwhile, women strive to ape the male stereotype. They drink, smoke and treat sex like fast-food, gobbling it up like free chop suey. A survey carried out across four countries by an advertising agency found that men in their twenties wanted to wait for four or five dates before having sex. Women went for sex on the first or second date. This is commonly called 'laddishness' but you could equally call it 'kamikaze' behaviour. Above all, today's woman is strident. She clamours to be heard – and men hear her, loud and clear. Today's female in full cry is the best laxative known to man.

If this posing by both sexes brings satisfaction, let alone happiness, why are the internet and the lonely-hearts ads filled with yearning? Look behind the 'Raunchy female, up for anything' façade and there is a woman desperate to be loved. Men offer what they think women want, but 'Stylish, affluent City type, fond of dining and travel' is probably a lowly clerk, dieting and on zit-watch in his lonely bed-sit. Modern research tells us that significant numbers of men are anxiety-ridden, and few consider themselves carefree.

The day of the rampant male is over.

I believe men and women are psychologically and

emotionally the same. Take away physical difference, strip them of centuries of conditioning, and they are nearer to peas in a pod than Martians and Venusians. The rate of change within society has accelerated in the last half-century. As old precepts and taboos fall by the wayside, mere mortals can't stand the pace. Now a woman can command a platoon, or a man wear a sarong, but only if they have the courage to challenge their respective stereotypes – and there is an industry dedicated to keeping those stereotypes alive.

Why do so many people seem afraid of men and women really getting together? Especially when so much evidence suggests that both sexes are desperate for lasting relationships?

The statement 'Finding someone to love and love us is the most important thing in life' was ticked as true for almost three-quarters of women and men questioned in a survey carried out by *The Times*. The proportion who believed it possible 'to be in love with one person for life' was almost equally as high.

So much for the belief that woman craves stability while man wishes merely to impregnate anything with a pulse.

If men and women could deal with the fact that they share the same fears and are fuelled by the same desires, then their chances of getting their act together would be multiplied tenfold. Instead, authors conspire to tell them they come from different species or inhabit different planets. Books on how to 'understand that strange alien you sleep with' abound. Any moment soon bridal shops will sell handbooks on the inevitability of divorce because you don't speak a common language.

We're told that only women can understand women, and only men can empathize with the hellishness of being male. Now, instead of complementing each other, the sexes are told to soldier on, always with the implied threat that one day, sperm will be unnecessary and men redundant. How long before both sexes can imagine men being *extinct*?

And if this were to happen, how would women fare in an all-female society? Any working woman will tell you that sisterhood isn't all it was cracked up to be. Again, research has revealed that the majority of career women thought female colleagues were their worst enemies in the workplace. Most even said they would prefer a male boss.

The truth is that women are no more accepting of potential rivals than men are. Behind the veil they are not only as smart as men, they are every bit as as ruthless. To suggest they're not is to perpetuate the 'weaker sex' image that held women back for centuries. The old idea that a woman was too gentle to have claws is out. Today her claws may be French-manicured, but they can still scratch.

Similarly, when stripped of the necessity to be 'manly', men can be as intuitive as women, just as bitchy, equally touchy but also just as compassionate. In other words, there are as many differences *within* the sexes as there are between them.

My hope is that nothing and no one will halt the emergence of men and women who may be physically different but are one in thought and feeling. Let's hear no more of 'it's a guy thing' or 'women are like that'; those phrases are simply excuses for bad behaviour. For a while the sexes must struggle, Houdini-like, with the shackles of convention and conditioning. Gurus may still chant that men and women are different species and never the twain shall meet… Rubbish! The meeting may yet be a long way off, but when it comes, my guess is that it will be sweet!

Until then, men and women must muddle through, Screwed Up, Bored And Desperate though we may be. This book looks at the frustration and bewilderment of the SUBAD generation as we struggle free from the cocoon. Its aim is to allow each sex to see how the other thinks and feels. In the end, it's men and women themselves who will decide whether or not they think and feel as one. I can hardly wait.

Communication
Why no one listens anymore

HE SAYS... This is supposed to be the age of communication, but as far as women are concerned, you could stick a 'non' in front and be more accurate.

Women never say what they mean. You spend months, even years, before you unlock the code. For example, 'It doesn't really matter' actually means 'It matters so much I'll leave you if you don't do it/say it/make it happen'.

Women have a passion for analysis when it comes to words. They ask, 'Is everything OK?' You say 'fine' which seems a perfectly straightforward word to me.

Does it satisfy them? Does it hell!

'What do you mean by fine? Finer than you felt before? Finer than it was with her? Fine as in "better" or fine as in "can't be improved"?'

I mean, fine is fine. If it wasn't fine you'd be out of there. You're with her, so what more is there to say?

And then there are the key words: 'love', 'commitment', 'marriage', 'future'. Women act like those words are some sort of mantra. I swear you could treat a woman like a football and as long as you kept chanting 'love and commitment' she'd take it.

Why can't they see you INTEND to say or do all those things? You just need a bit of time to get around to them. In the female vocabulary, however, 'commitment' comes after 'hello'. Just introducing yourself implies a bond – and that's scary.

Women need constant reassurance about the way they look, but they never ask outright. They say 'I look awful, don't I?' or 'I shouldn't have worn this'.

God help you if you say anything that suggests agreement. They want vehement denial of what they've just suggested.

How twisted is *that*?

'Anyone who isn't confused really doesn't understand today's situation'

And it's not just the 'does my bum look big' bit. They need the teeth, tits, shoes, 'shall I go blonde or Titian' stuff round the clock.

Any fool could work out that if they looked like a dog, you'd be long gone.

I suppose the difference between men and women is a question of fantasy. A growing boy's fantasy is freedom to roam. An adolescent girl's is roses round the door, you inside and the key on a chain round her neck. Except that nowadays you have to wear an apron and welcome her home from the office with new-baked bread.

The shame is that, if we're given time, we're really into the roses round the door thing. And the kids. (Not the new-baked bread, though, unless we can have one of those new machines that does it all …)

'If what you say is too cryptic,
it's probably meaningless.'

Most women are high-maintenance – which means you can't relax for a second. Gaze into space for thirty seconds and they pounce. 'What's wrong? There must be something wrong? What have I done?'

To keep the peace you have to appear enthusiastic, nod all the time and refrain from belching or yawning, when, really, just being able to switch off with them is the greatest possible compliment. You feel so good about them you don't feel moved to PERFORM.

And then they go and spoil it all.

One word to watch out for is 'nothing'. She's silent for five minutes. You ask what's up, and she says 'Nothing!'

Search your conscience. Have you neglected to walk the dog, take out the trash, put up some shelves? If you've forgotten one of those things, you're in the doghouse. Two of them and your clothes will be tossed out of the window and the locks changed.

Another danger zone is FAT. FAT is the bear in the woods as far as women are concerned. Say something harmless like 'You're OK as you are' and all hell breaks loose. Believe it or not, that simple remark is seen as an insult. In womanspeak it means 'You're a mess but there's nothing to be done about it'. And don't say 'That dress makes you look slim'. This will be construed as 'You're fat, but that dress makes you look marginally less fat'.

Beware, too, the direct question. 'Do you want to sleep with me?' is a minefield. Unless all your testosterone suddenly drained through your big toe, of course you want to sleep with her, but say 'yes' (the honest answer) at your peril. You will be told that all men are the SAME, after ONE thing and should be shipped to a penal colony on Alpha Zero. Lie through your teeth out of good manners and say 'No' and the heavens will open. 'What's wrong with me? Why don't you fancy me? You should have told me I wasn't your type' – and on and on. Say 'I might' and you'll still get the runaround.

It doesn't matter that her bookshelves are full of chick lit: no matter how much she comes on to you at first, every woman sees herself as straight out of the pages of Jane Austen.

Perhaps the most dangerous word of all is FEEL. 'How do you *feel*?' she'll say. You say 'OK' and she says 'No, how do you REALLY feel?' or even worse 'What do you feel like doing?' Tell the truth – that you feel like watching telly – and she will RECOIL. You'll get a lecture on insensitivity and have to rush to the all-night garage for flowers.

And this is what I don't understand: how a word like FEEL can reduce a clever woman to an obsessive. By day she lectures on particle physics or flies for BA, by night she conducts interrogation into the finer points of FEEL.

No wonder the life span of the male is shorter than the female. We succumb to the third degree.

The truth is, men are too straightforward to understand women and the one man who figured it out died laughing before he could pass on the secret.

OK, I'm making bad jokes about it, but the fact is I *want* to understand her. I'd like to get inside her mind and know what really makes her tick. It's just that I doubt she'll ever let me. She talks a lot but she doesn't really SAY anything.

SHE SAYS... When dealing with men, translation is the name of the game. Take that well-worn phrase 'my wife doesn't understand me'. It really means: 'My wife doesn't understand me but she knows me only too well'.

'Your guess is as good as mine' means 'Why the hell should I explain?' and suggests he's pissed-off. 'Fine' means 'not fine at all' – unless it's said absent-mindedly while he's trying to unhook your bra.

'I've got my reasons' is another cop-out. Interpret it as 'I shouldn't have done it but what's it got to do with you?'

Then there are pleas. 'I can't find it' means 'Find it for me'. 'What did I do this time?' is the old attack-as-the-best-means-of-defence ploy. If he says it piteously, he hopes you'll back off. If belligerently, he hopes to scare *you* into backing off.

'I'll fix it later' is tricky because it has two possible interpretations: 'If I leave it you might do it' and 'I don't know how to do it and don't want you to know that'. Either way, it's quicker (and probably cheaper) to call in a tradesman.

Now all this ducking and diving is annoying but the real rub is that we need to *talk*. Not chat, not engage in witty repartee but talk with our defences down. Talk that means 'Let's each of us see exactly where the other one is coming from'. The way I see it, a man and a woman could go through life together without either of them really knowing the other person and that's sad.

It's not as though women want a lot from men: a few kind words; a little appreciation; a sharing of feelings… But ask for reassurance and all you get is 'I'm not the romantic type', or even worse, 'You know I can't say things like that'.

Well, yes he can. He has a tongue. He thinks. He can say 'Will you iron my rugby shirt?' quick enough.

'Making them see the answer is easy. It's getting them to see the problem that's difficult.'

Men are also crap at compliments. You spend hours – positively *hours* – choosing the right jacket. When he sees you, he says 'Great shoes! And you haven't changed out of your flip-flops yet.

Inarticulateness is man's greatest drawback. I mean, given the chance, who would you rather be shipwrecked with: a stud with a six-pack and a six-word vocabulary or a man who could say 'I love you' in fourteen languages? All right you'd pick the stud, but think of the eventual boredom, whereas learning new languages could be a lot of fun when the breadfruit ran out.

The sad thing is that BAD men are never inarticulate. Lies gush out like North Sea oil: 'I didn't forget your birthday, but the card shop caught on fire.' Untruths like 'Sex is not important to me' come with practised ease. The fact is, sex is like oxygen. He can't take it or leave it.

For women, talking is nearly as good as copulating. Better in some cases. Men (unless they're habitual liars) behave as if God only gave them so many words and they have to save some for their old age. Ask if they love you and they'll say 'Of course'. Ask for a reason why they love you and lip-paralysis sets in. 'Why am I special?' will be met with 'Because you're you' – a meaningless *shibboleth* if I ever heard one – which makes you want to force him to sleep in the shed.

When they do speak, you still need an interpreter. 'I don't want to see you again' comes out as 'You're too good for me' or 'I don't want to tie you down'.

The very worst men just don't ring.

How chicken is *that*?

And once you're deep into a relationship, you're still deciphering. If he throws down his briefcase and says

'Don't mention work', it means he wants to tell you – IN FINE DETAIL – just what a jerk he has for a boss.

Even after long acquaintance, men are constitutionally incapable of saying 'I don't know'. They'll say 'That's not the point' or 'You *would* ask that' or 'Look at it this way' but 'I am a stupid berk who doesn't know B from a bull's foot' is just not in their vocabulary.

It's easy to work out that men can't find the right words because they can only operate one organ at a time, and the penis wins hands down, you can be. Yet get them on a favourite topic and you can't shut them up. The man who can't say 'I adore you', (three simple words), can expound for hours on the offside rule. Steer them to the latest video game and their vocabulary is *gynormous*.

> *'The most repeated phrase in the English language is "What's on telly?"'*

Yes, trivial things they can bang on about all night.

But ask them something like 'Do we have a future?' and they're struck dumb. If you press them on why they can't answer a simple question, they'll say 'It's a guy thing' – which isn't even logical. I mean, look at Aristotle and Socrates.

Years ago men wrote love poems and sentimental letters. They proposed on one knee and likened their women to April skies. Now it's a text message: 'Hope U R on 4 2nite'.

And this in 'the age of communication'!

Don't assume he or she will have your capacity for expression. Some people are more vocal than others. Repeatedly asking for vocal reassurances makes that reassurance less and less likely to materialize, and if you eventually force it out, what use will it be? If, by their actions, lovers demonstrate love, do words matter? If they don't demonstrate affection, do words count? Remember, if you stick around long enough, you'll eventually master their 'language' – just as they will master yours.

Ego

Ego is to planet as genitalia is to atom

HE SAYS… When you take away what a man is born with and what his mother made him, all that is left is ego – or so the saying goes. But what is ego? To some it's a dirty word. Big-head, know-all… you've heard the names. In fact, in most of us the ego is a small thing, shrinking, fragile, easily wounded. That's why we soon learn to bluster for Britain. We learn the art in order to throw a cordon around our weak spot.

In truth, we are terrified.

The male ego needs constant feeding. That's why women have more imagination than men: they need it in order to list men's good points. Well, that's what they tell us. And according to the state of your ego, you're liable to believe them.

The ego is supposedly situated in the brain. With some men, though, it slips and can be located in built-up shoulders or a six-pack or (more often) in the long, shiny bonnet of a high-powered car. That's where we excel: behind the wheel (open-top preferably). So wind in the hair, pair of Raybans, someone tasty in the passenger seat...

We walk with the Gods – or *drive* with them if you want to get picky.

Academics are above such trivia. Their ego resides in their superior knowledge and, boy, is it *some* ego. When wounded, it screams like a stuck pig and retribution follows. If I come back, I'm coming back as a don. Forget Olympic gold: the groves of academe is where true power resides.

That's another thing about the male ego. We think almost everyone else is superior, especially blokes with an education. Oh, we don't let on, but it's there, niggling.

'A thick skin is a gift from God.'

The interesting thing about the male ego is that it manifests late. Your average eight-year-old male stands in awe of his female counterpart. I had to share a textbook with a girl in Year Three and she never let me see it once. Can you blame us that, ten or fifteen years on, we kid ourselves that she exists to serve our needs?

Why the change? Well, men can pee standing up, have more control of their lachrymal glands and get fewer headaches than women. On the other hand, we are constitutionally incapable of caring for plants, and go completely to pieces if abandoned in lingerie departments because we don't know where to put our eyes.

'What will you be if you grow up?'

So what nurtures the male ego and effects such an apparent transformation? Mothers play a big part; all mothers are Jewish when it comes to their 'boys'. Employers, too, tend to play up male talents. But it is women who have traditionally contributed most, flocking round seemingly unworthy men as though that was all they were born to do.

Today's woman doesn't need to do that because she can provide for herself – which explains why today's men tend to be nervous wrecks.

The very word 'man' feeds the ego. 'Manly' is a compliment. 'Masculine' has a ring, too, and is more genteel than 'macho'. 'You're a big boy now – a *man*,' your mum says, and you square your little chest. The male myth also feeds the male ego. Superman, Spiderman, Batman: super-heroes all. Where is their female equivalent?

The operative word here is 'myth'. The male ego is easily withered, especially by a woman (well, *this* man's is anyway…).

That anxious 'Was that alright for you?' is not a polite question; it's a cry from the heart. Say 'I suppose so', or 'Uh huh', and you condemn us to lie awake, staring down the dark, trying to choose between penis enhancement or Viagra.

Men are born young and most of them die that way, cherishing their sense of self, kidding themselves that they are masters of situations which are really conceived and controlled by the woman in their life.

Which makes it all the more surprising that, when the occasion demands, they find the courage to acquit themselves like heroes.

SHE SAYS… Women are said to have less ego than men. I mean, when women feel bad they go shopping. Men invade someone else's country.

But this could be changing. We are waking up to the probability that Superman was not one whit more powerful than Superwoman. He was simply packaged differently.

In the past, a woman's ego was fed by two springs: beauty and power. Either could give you control.

Today's woman may rely on looks to get her to the interview, but it is her intellect that secures her seat on the board. Once there. her ego is more resistant than a man's. She will lie, steal and cheat where necessary. She will never surrender. 'I rule' is lettered through today's female executive like 'Blackpool' is through rock.

We still want to look our best, but appearance is no longer the only tool in our box.

We can compete – and we *like* it.

'It pays to conceal how much you think of yourself and how little you think of the other person'

Some vestiges of the past remain. Today's top female will still keep the pantry filled. I factor in the supermarket run alongside meetings and reviews. I remember a subordinate's birthday or take a duster to my desk if it needs it, but I have a stronger sense of my own power than a man in a similar position. His path to the top was eased by tradition. I fought for my place and therefore hold it by right.

Strangely enough, conventional beauty does little for the female ego. OK, we're glad we don't look like gargoyles and we dress well, but appearance is of secondary importance.

What matters is status, power, an office befitting your station and a retinue at least two persons larger than that of your rival.

'The Greeks had a word for it.'

Grooming is important. Where a male will, as soon as he is able, buy his shirts from Turnbull and Asser and order handmade shoes, the female ego demands an expensive haircut and a designer bag. When I clutch my Prada I feel strong.

But the healthy ego has no need of a plethora of designer labels. It knows its worth, so if the day comes I have to downgrade, I'll do it and move on.

As yet women do not have that sense of sex that enables them from birth. To be born a man is to be born to privilege. To be born a woman is still a stumbling block – something to be surmounted.

I remember the moment it dawned on me that women were the 'second sex'. I didn't like it then and I won't tolerate it now, but it still exists, hidden away. 'A man's job, get a man to do it' … it will take time for those mantras to go – but go they will.

The rare male expresses his ego through his home. A woman always does.

Where a man will call in an expert, to design a room, a woman still builds a nest, even if she no longer hand-sews her curtains.

I still do things for myself if I can. Inside me there is this desire to create, to nest-build, but neither of those emotions is as strong as the desire to be Number One.

In rows, the female ego erupts. I can wield my tongue like a sword. When I'm finished, nothing of my opponent remains. Afterwards I cringe, remembering all those admonitions to 'be pleasant, be nice, be a good girl'.

When the day comes that this doesn't bother me I'll know I've overcome my conditioning and ego is now rampant but not out of control.

Where women are concerned, we are still a decade or two away from that.

Deal with it

Ego is the engine that powers us to achieve, yet it is as fragile as a leaf-bud. In some people it grows to gigantic proportions, nourished by self-induced myths. In others it can shrivel. Prize your ego – it is what makes you what you are – but never overfeed it. Don't seek to impose it on others; they have their own. Beware of people whose egos are out of control, and nurture those whose egos are underdeveloped. Never seek to damage someone else's ego. When you do that, you only succeed in damaging your own.

Alphas
Power games have leather accessories

HE SAYS… There is a male hierarchy. We don't talk about it but each one of us knows our place in the pecking order, and although some of us are keen to move, the rest of us quite like our lowly state.

Top of the tree is the Alpha male. It's easy to pick him out. He will be taller than anyone else. Ever since mankind walked erect, being erecter than most has mattered – which is why some of us resort to shoe lifts. These are hidden heels inside the shoe which can add a comfortable inch to a man's stature. Go much further than that and you resemble someone clumping along in diver's boots and look a proper Charlie.

Not that your genuine Alpha would resort to such measures. If he is not naturally tall, he will be very small indeed. Alphas don't do anything in medium. Though short, he will be dominant: think Napoleon or Danny de Vito.

If you're Alpha you're always a team captain – if not team captain, then you bunk off all sport and affect to despise it. Correction, an Alpha would *really* despise it.

Alphas must be CHIEFS, they are constitutionally incapable of being Indians. If they cannot be chiefs they will be INDIVIDUALS.

And they can speak with authority on any subject as soon as they sprout facial hair.

The rest of us look on in envy and plot just how to bring them down but you never try it. You know it would be a waste of time. Occasionally one comes a cropper and then the rest of us give an inward cheer but it stays inward. Alphas have a nasty habit of bobbing up again if down.

'Even his urine is château-bottled.'

One way of spotting an Alpha is to notice which way he faces in a communal shower. Alphas always face OUTWARDS. Nervously facing the wall or hiding under a towel is not for them. They never compare the size of their organ – they know it's twice the size of anyone else's, even if folded in half.

They are likely to end up as politicians because they are capable of talking for hours with complete conviction on subjects about which they know nothing. They also know forty-two different methods of avoiding a direct question. If they don't choose politics, they opt for the law or publishing.

Both these professions allow them to be lordly, an essential Alpha characteristic.

Now you may ask why I, being so knowledgeable, don't put that knowledge into practice and become an Alpha. It's because I know my place. I am a foot soldier: a good man in a crisis but strictly B material. Don't ask me to explain it, but inside yourself you just know where you stand – and an Alpha I'm not.

For example, I like to get on with people. Your true Alpha isn't afraid of being unpopular. Indeed, he regards it as part of the job. Being popular is not what matters. What matters is being in *authority*.

'Possessing animal magnetism isn't a crime, surely?'

Women are attracted to Alpha males. Brimming over with confidence makes for charisma. Alpha males do not have a self-doubting bone in their body, ergo they are charismatic. Usually they have wit and élan, which they learned at public school or picked up by example (élan is one of the few advantages of an expensive education).

Short Alphas substitute 'forceful' for 'charismatic' and 'bloody domineering' for 'élan'. They usually have a Brummie or Glaswegian accent and glance menacingly from side to side.

Tall or short, Alphas are leaders of the pack, a position most women find knee-weakeningly attractive. (I'm your average five-nine so that's another reason why I can't be an Alpha...)

With women, an Alpha male will be seductive and aloof by turns. If she succumbs, her new lord and master will observe her devotion with a curious detachment, rather as a cat contemplates a newly caught mouse.

The good news is that Alphas seldom eat their prey.

The bad news is they can get any woman they want and it's usually the woman of *your* dreams.

Alpha males are never attracted to Alpha women. Nor do bimbos appeal to them. They want intelligent, personable women who are attractive enough to exhibit but compliant enough to be handmaidens.

If they marry them (and this is strictly a question of being the one in place when the Alpha decides to mate), they will be elegantly fed and watered and otherwise ignored. Winning a prize in the village art competition will always be smiled upon. Writing a ground-breaking thesis on 'How to deal with Fiscal Collapse' will not.

There can only be one Alpha in an Alpha family.

There is a myth that every Alpha male is looking for the perfect woman. On the contrary, Alphas feel that by conferring on their women the status of being 'their women', they render the most ordinary female perfect. The Alpha male will make sure his woman has everything – but everything she has will be of *his* choosing.

The most the rest of us can hope for is that we get their leavings, but when that happens you live with the knowledge that your woman wanted Alpha and had to settle for beta.

Some women shun Alphas. Don't ask me why, but they do. These women are RARE creatures and to be prized.

Alpha men have few real friends. Their forte is acolytes and acquaintances. Whatever they join they will quickly become chairman or captain of, but while people look up to Alphas they have no desire to be their best mates.

Alphas never raise their voices, not even on the mobile phone. Unless they are short Alphas, in which case they shout a lot. Most of my working life has been spent in the shadow of Alphas; I speak whereof I know. The clothes of Alpha males never crease.

Neither do Alphas sweat, unless on the sports field, in which case their sweat is odourless and non-staining.

In this, as in everything, Alphas reign supreme.

When, eventually, they are ousted from the boardroom, or the dutiful wife deserts, they take up conservation or train for the Church as late entrants. They seldom remarry and their offspring show a strong desire to live abroad.

'If you're not talking about an Alpha,
they're not listening.'

Though surrounded by followers, Alphas tread a lonely road and that's a consolation for the rest of us. In the pub, with the lads, knowing there'd be genuine grief if we popped our clogs, we may dream wistfully of being Alpha – but that's all it amounts to.

Alphaland is a lonely place.

SHE SAYS… Alpha females don't walk. They *prowl*, thrusting forward their hips, taking long strides… their body language says 'Follow that!'

Sure enough, ordinary women quail before them.

Men are aroused by them, but seldom marry them – unless they have the victim gene, in which case God help them!

Colleagues loathe and fear them, bosses promote them, but are curiously unmoved if it becomes commercially sensible to sack them.

Alpha females have no friends.

'An Alpha can strut sitting down.'

So how do you become an Alpha? It begins in school. Alphas are leaders of the pack while still pig-tailed. They bully but only psychologically. If force is required they have hench-women to do the necessary. Their role is to stand immobile while the protractor point is driven into your shrinking thigh. They may utter a lordly 'Had enough?' But that's all.

Their real power is actually difficult to define, but it is unmistakable. Those in an Alpha's favour bask in intense sunlight. To be outside her orbit is unthinkable. Even her victims respect her. They may wish she would dematerialize, but they never question her magnetism.

Alpha females are unique. They neither need nor

want support. Neither does the Alpha feel allegiance to her sex. Indeed, she may well treat other women more harshly than a man in the same situation.

Alpha females show no mercy.

Nor do they expect forbearance. They must always be in control, ahead of the game – which means they must never display weakness, fear or indecision, which makes sex tricky! An Alpha is incapable of lying back and thinking of England. If she thinks of anything during sex, it is how to extricate herself from it while still in full sail. Alphas never scramble for the bathroom or huddle inside the duvet so their wobbly bits won't show. If she must walk naked, she walks tall. Cellulite dare not settle there.

Although Alphas always occupy premier position, they are not necessarily the sharpest tool in the box. Their rise is due to a combination of qualities other than mere intelligence. Self-confidence, determination, venom and ruthlessness form a powerful mix.

Somehow Alphas take the inside track and stick there, seeing off all challengers. Eventually, it becomes a given that they reign supreme and challengers fall away.

They share one thing with Alpha males: they *never* discuss. Why bother when the decision is theirs alone and they've already made it? When talking to their workforce they operate the KISS principle (*Keep It Simple, Stupid*). They lay out what they want and expect it to happen.

The men who employ them spend a lot of time trying to figure out how and why they came to value them so much. At what point did the Alpha's opinion become Holy Writ? Why do they fear the wrinkling of an Alpha's brow, the almost imperceptible moue of distaste that is her only sign of emotion? Her secret is partly sexual, partly a triumph of will – hers over yours. You fear she may despise you and it renders you impotent.

Female colleagues regard her as a ball-breaker but she seldom, if ever, reduces a man to a ball-broken wreck. That is because she seldom needs to do so.

Similarly, she never boasts. What comes to her comes as a right so why proclaim it?

Although she is usually good-looking and always impeccably turned out, she is seldom surrounded by men, as Alpha males are by woman. Men may admire her, even lust after her – but when it comes to choosing a partner they prefer someone who will laugh at their jokes and be, if they're honest enough to admit it, just a little bit dumb. Men need women who give them confidence.

Alpha females make men realize their own shortcomings. They may marry, but it seldom works, unless the man is Alpha, too, and travels on business a lot. If there are children they will be Alpha from birth but curiously detached. When unmarried Alpha women step down, they take with them a more than golden handshake and afterwards reign in a circle of soroptomist friends. There is a large attendance at their funerals, but few cry.

Deal with it

Inside all of us is the desire to be Alpha. That desire is commonly called ambition and it has its place. When it gets out of hand, when being Number One becomes not an aspiration but an imperative, it's easy to get things out of proportion. True Alphas make doubtful friends and difficult lovers. They can dazzle – but are they dependable? If you aim to be Alpha, what else have you to offer in love and friendship? The art of living is surely to marry ambition with real quality of life – and that takes a great deal of thought and effort.

Body Image
How to turn a frog into a toad

HE SAYS... In childhood you don't think too much about your appearance. If no one calls you 'Potato Head', you rub along.

And then one day it hits you.

You are a nerd, a geek, the original eight-stone weakling, in addition to which you have Prince Charles's ears, Hitchcock's belly, incipient acne and an eye in the middle of your forehead.

For a while you hide away, working out how to turn the frog into a prince.

Where to start?

You are too short, too slight, too mousey, your complexion would put a macaroon to shame; the absence of a single redeeming feature sears your soul. Shoe lifts, chest wigs, acne cream that could strip paint … you contemplate them all. You even dally with penis extension but chicken out.

A magazine tells you that 'Metrosexual man' is the new king of the jungle, opting for high-maintenance grooming products which go far beyond the basic repertoire of soap, water and zit cream.

The secret is to see little contradiction between masculinity and vanity. So you buy products until the bathroom shelf collapses under their weight. You become a sucker for celebrity sponsorship. If someone who is a household name (even if only in his own household), tells you in print that cow-dung face-packs work, you disappear beneath a slather of manure.

'We're not all beautiful.
Some of us are hardly presentable.'

Encouraged by the results you venture out, but when you catch sight of yourself in the mirror behind the bar you still look like an otter and take an early bath. At work you make like Quasimodo on the principle that if you are ugly, then be the ugliest.

Then the tea lady takes pity on you. 'You're a nice lad', she says, slipping you an Eccles cake, 'but your hair lets you down'.

Eureka! You spend the next two nights in front of your mirror, sucking in your cheeks and trying to decide between a French crop and a public-school flick. The next day you visit a salon. The stylist picks up a lank lock and eyes it with distaste.

'What,' his expression says 'am I supposed to do with *this*?'

You shrink into the chair while he extols the virtues of mullets, fins, shags or spikes. You are reduced to a gibbering wreck by this amount of choice and signal for him to get on with it. He lops, bleaches, colours, deconstructs and gels until you emerge, blinking, under an orange halo and with a hole in your wallet.

It takes two weeks and a litre of shampoo to restore a semblance of normality.

'To look good you must be prepared to suffer.'

In the meantime you've taken out a loan to buy a Paul Smith suit guaranteed to cover all deficiencies and there's a brief moment of euphoria when you read that baldness really *is* associated with virility. Baldness you can aspire to. You search your scalp for a brief patch of pink, but in spite of the recent depredations there is nothing but luxuriant growth.

The same applies to your body hair. Legs and back, it springs eternal. You see a picture of Becks smooth as a baby's bottom and enrol for a full body wax.

Your eyes water for a week, which is how long it takes the re-growth to start. You contemplate a Brazilian next time but cry off when you hear you have to bite on a tongue depressor to dull the pain.

And then it hits you (again). When did Schwarzenegger worry about his short back and sides? How does Beckham wow the women with a voice like a constipated canary? Six-packs, that's how! Pecs appeal! You enrol at a gym and throw yourself into a fitness regime.

You're an eight-and-a-half-stone weakling when you read that man's greatest asset is his smile. Not a car-salesman's rictus or a bank manager's smirk; a real, college heart-throb, head-back, crinkle-eyed, 42-carat grin.

You try it in the rear-view mirror and realize your teeth resemble old dominos.

The orthodontist supplies you with a contraption like a boxer's gum shield, which you fill with whitening gel and clamp to top and bottom sets each night, wondering if your lips will split and leave you fit only for a freak show. Six weeks and £750 later you have gnashers in a delicate shade of taupe which the dentist declares blinding white… but it doesn't blind him to the fact that you've post-dated the cheque.

You perfect a technique of drawing back your lips to reveal your new smile – until you hear a colleague refer to you as Hannibal Lecter.

Depressed, you buy a self-help book entitled *How to Stand Out in a Crowd*. It advocates licking your lips and preening. Preening necessitates tossing your head and lengthening your neck. You practice licking and preening to a mirror until the resemblance to a gecko becomes too much to bear. But you do take note of the dominance chapter. This urges men to stand with feet six to ten inches apart and toes pointing outward.

You should also wear bulkier clothing and square your shoulders.

Next time out you lick, preen, square and bulk, but find you can only manage two at a time. You settle for squaring and preening until your sister slips you the card of a website for nervous habits.

So you decide that clothes, not manners, really maketh man and aim for the eccentric look. This means ditching anything with a label and wearing a stripy tank top, drainpipe jeans and your old school blazer. You add chunky specs and carry a well-thumbed Stephen Hawking under your arm.

And suddenly the geek is king!

Women flock to you and all you have to do is sport a 'Save the Rainforest' badge. The master-stroke is when you trade your Audi for an old Citroën 2CV. Women besiege you, seriously handsome men beg to know your secret. You smile an enigmatic smile, touch your nose and preen a little bit.

Let them find out the hard way, like you did!

'Does my bum…?' 'Yes, it does.'

SHE SAYS… Image is everything on a first date. You want to look relaxed (which you're not) and not as though you've spent the last six hours agonizing over what to wear (which you have).

You picture his eyes lighting up at the sight of you in your floaty chiffon – and then discover it's a two-mile hike across fields to his local. When, shivering, you say goodbye, you resolve never again to put your faith in clothes.

So you do a 'Mirror, mirror on the wall' session. Why are you so dependent on clothes? Answer: you *hide* behind them. Henceforth you must learn to love yourself and your body and put clothes where they belong: in the wardrobe. If you don't love yourself, how can you expect anyone else to love you?

On the other hand, how can anyone love someone with the legs of a Welsh pit pony and beanbag thighs? So you diet. F-plan, C-plan, G… you name it, you try it.

Your cheeks sink but your backside remains.

You contemplate a face-lift, but a kind friend suggests it would threaten your fragile sense of identity. Learning that your sense of identity is fragile does you no good at all. Particularly as the kind friend in question has a killer body and immovable mascara.

'I'm tired of all this beauty-is-only-skin-deep trash. Who wants a beautiful spleen?'

Your own mascara comes off if you cry, shower or swim but resists any attempt to remove it at bedtime.

So you decide to go golden. You step inside a booth and a disembodied voice tells you how to move arms and legs to achieve maximum coverage. As soon as you're arranged to the voice's satisfaction, a mist envelops you, there's the whirr of a dryer and seconds later you look like a citizen of Sierra Leone.

This is a snip at £20 – until the voice tells you it will last a week. Fifty-two times £20, or £1,040 a year.

For that kind of money you could *move* to Sierra Leone.

While you're pondering your next step, a succession of whip-thin women hog the headlines. Liz Hurley, who never eats at all; Jemima Khan, who looks anorexic; and Davina McCall, who, after two pregnancies, could be threaded through the eye of a needle and bellows for Britain.

You take stock of yourself. Boobs pendant, stomach sagging, ankles... your ankles are the root cause of your inferiority complex. Do they Botox ankles? And how would new ankles fit with pit-pony legs?

So you decide to begin with your hair. It's a well-known fact that men hate women to cut their hair. Husbands who wouldn't notice if their wives sat with a brown paper bag over their head will bridle like stallions at the mention of a cut and trim. This stems from the days when men dragged off their women by the hair, but hey: this is the new millennium.

Your body, your hair, your decision.

You go for a Joan of Arc crop and hide in the spare room for a week till it begins to grow. You're still cowering when a woman on *Richard and Judy* says that a warm smile is an international signal of friendliness.

You've always fancied a foreign boyfriend, so you start to smile *a lot*. You also take to throwing back your hair – until you remember it was swept up and put in a pedal bin. Thereafter you stick to smiling.

And then one night on Channel Four they screen *Basic Instinct*. You watch Sharon Stone cross her legs and struggle to see what everyone said was visible but you have never managed to catch. You cross and uncross your own legs a few times and allow your shoe to dangle from your toe. You have a nice instep and this heartens you.

You also have great cleavage. You know this because men, especially your colleagues, seldom look anywhere else. Sometimes you think your voice must be coming from your left nipple, so rapt is their attention.

You buy built-up bras and treat yourself to a manicure, facial and pedicure. Every bit of you is zinging – but men still contemplate your left breast and mumble incoherently while doing so.

You start to worry. Are they transfixed by the magnificence of your cleavage, or is the rest of you so unpalatable that they can't bear to look?

Your best friend eats like a hippo and has the body of a greyhound. You are in inverse ratio. You don't eat for a week and then pig out on Marmite toast until you get spots round your mouth.

This is the last straw.

'If you have charm you don't need anything else.
If you don't have it nothing else works.'

You go in search of a burqa but succumb instead to a pair of Jimmy Choos. Even in your tatty old dressing gown these shoes make you look sensational. The pit-pony legs elongate, the ankles thin, the pelvis tilts, the neck rises proud from the Real Madrid shirt your ex left in the wash.

You realize that the arch of the foot has a potency that no other body part possesses. It is the ultimate erogenous zone. You have cracked the code. You put the Jimmy Choos on the mantelpiece, sit cross-legged on the hearthrug and worship.

Deal with it

Sometimes it can seem we inhabit one of those Halls of Mirrors at the circus. In this mirror you're fat; in that one you're thin. You contract or expand with each turn, your face relaxes into jelly or contracts to a grimace every second and you don't like what you see. In other words, what you see in the mirror is often an imprecise reproduction of what you are. Your reflection is filtered through your moods and, above all, your fears. So if you feel you resemble a badly assembled sofa or your nose would outdo Pinocchio, don't go into hiding; take advice. Ask the opinion of someone you trust or a professional. If they tell you that you look not only acceptable but good, believe them. If they agree you have problems, seek expert help in effecting change.

Flirting
Simply connect. Alternatively, screw the whole thing up

HE SAYS... Cavemen had it easy: first, slay your dinosaur then catch your woman, drag her off to your cave and do the business. After that you could scarper if you wanted to. If you were a NEW CAVEMAN you stuck around and nine months later you were a patriarch

Today it's more complicated. Slaying the dinosaur is the easy part. Dragging off your woman is well nigh impossible. She has to be WOOED.

And before you can woo, you have to FLIRT, which does not come easily to a real man.

I mean, men as a species are straightforward. Show them a sample and they'll buy. Women are contrary. Be too upfront and they're likely to slap you down just for the hell of it. Then they'll tell all their friends you harassed them and one day a woman you've never seen before, much less insulted, will call you a sexist pig.

The most important implement for flirting is the eye. Women bat their eyelids. Men don't do that unless they're in drag, in which case give them a wide berth.

With men it has to be the STARE – eye contact timed to the nanosecond.

First you look anywhere but at the woman in question; middle distance is what you should aim for. When that gets them curious – and it will, believe me – give them a fifteen-second blast with the old irises, brows slightly lifted, mouth unsmiling. Your eyes should lock with hers. If they don't, go back to the middle distance and start again.

If you do get a satisfactory lock, hold it until she's just about ready to drop her eyes then look away. Even stroll off. By the time you come back she'll have ascertained your name – Christian and pet – your occupation, marital status, interests, inside leg and mother's maiden name and be ripe for conquest.

Trust me. It never fails.

Except the times you realize she's not actually returning your gaze, she's looking past you to the bloke who's just walked in.

Or the time her enquiries turn up something off-putting, like the fact that you're a tax inspector or have '666' tattooed under your hairline. After that, you could stare at her till the cows came home and not get a nibble.

Once you've established the STARE and survived the vetting, the next step is TOUCHING. A hand on the arm, cupped under an elbow – you should feel electricity of some sort, which is her way of saying Welcome.

Sometimes, though, she'll use an alternative ploy. She'll be rude – *really* rude.

This is a good sign.

'A clever woman is a mirror which shows a man what he wants to see.'

If a woman can summon up the energy to tell you you're a scumball and should go forth and multiply, you're as good as stooping to enter the cave and she's a dead weight on your shoulder.

At times like that you realize there is a God.

This is when it pays to be cool. Breaking into a chorus of 'Bess, you is my woman now…' is not a good idea. The female psyche likes the chase.

When she insults you, say, 'If that's how you feel…' and move away. This gives her the chance to come over all contrite and beg forgiveness, like they do in the best black-and-white movies. She'll bat her eyelids and you'll accept her apology and suggest a truce.

All this takes about thirty-five minutes, but it's time well spent.

One note of caution: when using the STARE don't let the beam waver from the target or you may find you've pulled the tubby Goth with the six-inch fingernails.

Some men don't have the patience for flirting. They believe in storming the ramparts. You remember the old joke: 'You dancin'?' 'You askin'?' Nowadays it's 'My motor's racing. Your place or mine?'

This will get you either red-hot sex or a bed in A&E. Safer to stick to the STARE … or bat your eyelids – or your buttocks or any other body parts which can be pressed into service.

Just remember the SAS motto: Who Dares Wins!

SHE SAYS… Men are so vain that attracting their attention is easy. *Too* easy. Catch their eye by accident and they'll take it as a come-on. You're simply looking around…

OK, so you're talent-spotting but where's the harm in that?

Your eye lights on a guy and you take in the usual thing – age, height, hairstyle, teeth, fingernails; it doesn't take more than a second. But wait a quarter of a minim before you look away and they'll assume you're besotted with them and tell all their friends. Before you know it you'll be seen to be mad for him and up for it and your reputation will be up the archipelago.

Women aren't like that.

If a man looks at me, I don't see myself bearing his children (well, not immediately, anyway). The trouble is that even in the twenty-first century you need a technique for reeling in a seabass without catching a host of little minnows in your net.

Eyelid batting went out with whalebone. Nowadays women are supposed to be upfront. 'Ask outright' magazines tell you. 'Men like a woman to be direct.' But try as we might, inside today's woman is a Jane Austen type who wants to be sure of a welcome before she rings the bell.

I mean, even for a liberated woman, 'I'm yours. Take me' doesn't trip easily off the tongue when said to a complete stranger.

Short of being bold and saying 'Your place or mine?' – which I couldn't do for Colin Farrell, let alone the jerks you meet in the normal course of things – flirting is what you're left with.

I've found that the ricochet method can be effective. That's where you flirt with A in order to attract B. It will work very well except where A doesn't realize he's a foil and responds with enthusiasm to what he sees as a genuine come-on.

You sense B hovering over the horizon and you want to give him your full attention, but A is a limpet which latches on to your batting eyelids (yes, I know I said eyelid-batting was out but sometimes old methods are best) and refuses to be dislodged. I once had to go out with a guy for a month because he got in the way of a come-on intended for someone else.

*'When you can't think of anything to say,
rattle your jewellery.'*

Looking up at a man can be effective if you get in close enough. Just make sure he's not halfway through a dripping kebab when you tilt your head to look up his nostrils. I did that once and it was MESSY. If he's five-ten and you're five-four this will come naturally.

If he's five-six and you're five-nine, which I am, you have to resist the impulse to lie on the floor and look up the line of his trouser crease. Bending your knees a little, sticking out your butt and rounding your shoulders, then tilting your head does it.

Well, it does for me, but chiropractors don't come cheap.

But hell: what's a little pain?

Conversation can be a flirting aid. Beginning a sentence and leaving it to hang in the air works like a charm. 'I was just thinking...' said into space is a hook. He waits for a long moment, hoping you'll finish what you were saying. When you don't, he says, 'You were thinking *what*?' I don't answer. Instead, I smile enigmatically and shake my head a little.

Rueful is good. Sighing is great as long as it's subtle and not akin to a 'Harumph'. You can say 'Oh, it's nothing', but it's more impressive if you do it in French ('*C'est rien*')or Yiddish (*Ni to farvus*). I might have wound up with a rabbi using that one if his mother hadn't interfered.

Unfortunately, unless he's a linguist he may decide you're barking when you start speaking in tongues and go elsewhere. I've had that happen a few times.

I have to admit I enjoy flirting. It makes you feel good even when you wouldn't cross the road with the man in question. Unfortunately it works best with men who are twice your age.

Why do men employ mathematics in the chase? They take their age, divide it by their car number and multiply it by four and that's their target. I wonder sometimes what goes on inside their heads to make them think that when they can see female wrinkles we can't see theirs.

And fifty-year-olds in stressed-out jeans just sucks. If they kept their dignity we might give them house room in a sort of Cary Grant kind of way, but a wrinkly giving you high-fives is enough to kill the flirting impulse stone dead.

Also men and women use different translators when it comes to flirting. I mean, with us it's innocent – at the beginning, anyway. A man gives me the eye and I take it as mild interest. Nothing more. They take rapid eyelid movement as foreplay. Throw your hair back and they're reaching for a zip.

The narrow escapes I've had!

And if you try to explain you were merely testing the water, they make out you're the whore of Babylon.

If you were being sensible you wouldn't flirt at all, but think of the fun you'd miss. So, get batting and tilting but be discreet. A little gentility never comes amiss.

Deal with it

If flirting is obvious, it has already failed. Nothing is quite so off-putting as someone deliberately casting a line. Some people are natural flirts and have made an art of it. Enjoy them but don't take them too seriously. Beware people who see flirting as a means of accumulating scalps. If you want to cultivate someone and don't trust your ability to flirt, put them at their ease instead. People are attracted to others who make them feel good about themselves, and the best way of doing that is to feel good about yourself. Flirting comes easily to those who know they have something to offer. Confidence communicates itself but so does vulnerability; if you're shy, don't see it as a drawback but as a virtue. (Think about it. Don't you feel drawn to a vulnerable person?) So take account of all you have to offer and get cracking.

Dating
It's not for life, it's only an evening, for God's sake

HE SAYS… Once upon a time a date was a gooey sweetmeat which came in a coffin-shaped box. Nowadays it's an ordeal akin to surgery without anaesthetic.

There are five types: blind, speed, internet, organized or random. Random is the one where you fancy the colleague who is so proud of her 40DD she positively flourishes it. You ask if she'd like to go out for a drink and find yourself facing sexual harassment charges for eyeing her cleavage.

Asking outright used to work in your father's day, but progress and the courts have rendered it obsolete, so you must resort to other means. Your father met your mother when his Auntie Millie asked her to tea, but that was the Golden Age, when life was straightforward.

Now we live in Progressive times, which is French for 'Bloody Awkward'.

You consider internet dating but female pulchritude on the worldwide web could be an eighteen-stone docker from Hull who keeps crossbows on his wall. So you try a lonely-hearts ad because when you did speed dating you almost got arrested.

A friendly barmaid gives you a crash course in the jargon of the lonely heart, taking pity on you after you've scoured the columns for an hour without lifting your pint to your lips because one hand is scratching your head and the other tearing out your hair.

She makes it all plain. GSOH equals good sense of humour. NS is non-smoker, WLTM means would love to meet and OHAC means own house and car. So you're a M who is NS and has GSOH and OHAC. You should be home and dry.

'Mating is too serious to be left to chance.'

You word your ad carefully. 'Romantic, easygoing M, 30ish, WLTM warm-hearted F for friendship/ relationship. Must have GSOH and be NS. Animals accepted'. With any luck she'll have a Weimaraner and you've always wanted a Weimaraner.

On second thoughts you strike out 'romantic'. Mustn't raise expectations. On third thoughts 'easygoing' sounds too, well, easygoing. You substitute 'professional'. 'Warm-hearted?' That sounds motherly and what you're looking for is something else.

'Professional M 30ish WLTM fun-loving F.' 'Fun-loving?' She might come armed with sex-aids.

After two hours you decide it's easier to reply to one of the ads in the F section. But which one?

'Intelligent, voluptuous redhead seeks tactile, passionate M for fun?' 'Voluptuous?' Scary! You move on.

'Svelte, sassy, spirited F 32 5'10" seeks tall, sparky, self-aware soul mate'. Well, this one's certainly into alliteration – but 5'10"? You'd spend your life looking up to her, especially if she wore heels and that's what ruined the Charles/Diana marriage.

'Reason says love sucks. Instinct say "Yum, yum".'

In the end, you opt for 'Quirky blonde graduate, petite, seeks charming, educated M'. Well you are a B.Sc. On the other hand, 'quirky' could cover a multitude of sins…

You put aside the want ads and ponder the imponderability of the M/F relationship. Once upon a time women wanted a provider. If he didn't snore or pick his nose that was advantageous but not essential. Now that women earn their own money they can afford to be choosy.

Which is bully for them but hell for us.

She wants your body all right but sometimes it seems as though she'd like it hanging from a tree. Worse even than that, she tries to intellectually emasculate you.

Anyway, back to dating. The Greeks maintain that everyone has a soul mate. Find him or her and happiness is assured.

What the Greeks left out is that finding that soul mate is harder than finding the proverbial needle, and if you do find her, she may have other ideas.

So you go to dinner parties looking, hoping. You join political parties and go on camera courses or visit stately homes. Eventually your best friend fixes you up with a blind date. The first one spends the whole evening discussing good and bad carbs and tuts when you have pudding.

Undeterred when you tell him it's a no-no, he tries again. This one says nothing except 'Fancy!' to every statement you make.

The third one spends the whole night staring at the guy at the next table.

When your best friend goes to the loo, she disappears too and is a *long* time coming back. She lets you take her home, but when you ask for her phone number she says it's 'in the book'. So you ask for her surname because you only know her as Jodie. 'That's in the phone book, too,' she says. You're back in the taxi and halfway home before the penny drops.

So who needs women?

Some guru once said 'Man is incomplete until he's married – and then he's finished.' Dates are for the birds or for Christmas.

All the same, you'd like to tell those women advertising for love that if they want a really nice guy – GSOH, NS, OHAC *et al* – they should stop dating good-looking assholes.

SHE SAYS… It's something you talk about easily when you're twelve. Open *Bliss* or *Sugar* and they tell you how to date, when to date and how to use a date to bring a man to his knees. Once you're out of the teen-mag stage, dating becomes a jungle. Explore it at your peril.

The internet is full of women in search of the perfect date or bemoaning the Date from Hell. I mean, all you want is a pleasant evening – not a lifetime's commitment. As far as you can see, marriage is servitude without the appropriate remuneration.

OK, if love strikes across the bistro table you're as up for it as the next woman, but you're not expecting it, and the fact that you spent two hours getting ready and had a full body wax the day before is simply coincidence, nothing more.

But do men see it like that? Do they hell!

They think you're after a meal ticket or a notch on your Laura Ashley duvet.

The more paranoid think you carry a registry office application form in your handbag.

Little do they know that after what seems a lifetime of men who don't ring back, you've given up on meeting the man of your dreams. You've done all the obvious: boy next door, school chum, friend of a friend, matched by computer.

They SUCK.

You've even tried going for younger men on the basis that as none of them grow up anyway why bother about an age gap? All you have to show for hours of ennui and frustration is KNOWLEDGE.

For example, bald men try harder to please; men who dress well are gay (or at least ambivalent); and the idea that men can be strong, caring and loving at the same time is about as true as fish learning to ride bicycles.

You're single and cynical so you decide to get businesslike. You no longer hope for a soul-mate; you'll settle for a masculine presence in your life.

No strings. No complications.

'Never sleep with anyone whose troubles are worse than your own.'

So, henceforth you will date *purposefully*. You like that word 'purposeful'. It smacks of a woman who knows what she wants. You can do it in the workplace, you can do it here.

It's simply a matter of organization.

You divide dating into sections. Random: men you meet in the course of the day. Contrived: fixed by a friend, aka blind. Arranged: the back pages of *Private Eye* or surfing the net. And then there's speed – but you don't talk about that because it's too painful to remember.

Blind dates are just as bad.

'He's really nice, but don't mention sex,' your best friend says before a vicar walks into the room.

You don't see yourself as a vicar's wife and neither does he.

Besides, this guy has hands that cover more territory than Christopher Columbus. When he finds out your reflexes are better than his, he tells you he has to plan next Easter's services – and it's only July. Up until then you were rehearsing seven different ways of making sure you never saw him again.

So why must you quell the desire to run after him and demand a second chance? Is this what they call desperation? If so it's foolish. You've got years before you need to feel desperate (well, eighteen months at least…).

Random dates usually occur after a man you've known for years catches you feeling low. You've always managed to avoid him, now you say yes because it's better than hara-kiri, but your heart's not in it. He takes you to a nice restaurant but you order the cheapest thing on the menu because you don't want to be too beholden. The look in his eyes when you tell him every night is hair-wash night will haunt you for weeks.

For a little while you lick your conscience and then you decide to find the right guy by advertising. You give *Private Eye* a wide berth and opt for a really upmarket broadsheet.

Strangely, the language of the ads is no different to the *Eye* so you play along.

'Crazy F, 23 (which is only a little lie), WLTM slim professional 6ft actor, preferably called Pitt'.

Well, that's a non-starter so you try 'Taurean seeks Cancerian for settling down'.

Yuk!

'Blue-eyed brunette, early 20s (just another little lie) seeks cockerel to share eggs!'

Might as well be forthright.

In the end you give up writing your own and look at the male ads. This sounds promising. 'Solvent M, 30, medium build. Likes travel and cinema. OHAC, GSOH, NS, WLTM sun-kissed siren 20-45 for who knows what'.

You're about to lift the phone when reason prevails. '20 to 45'? He's casting a wide net, isn't he? And 'for who knows what?'

Which bit of *that* is reassuring?

You back off again. After all, a few months of celibacy never hurt. Sadie Shorter swore it cured her rosacea.

You order a video and a curry, snuggle into your oldest jimjams and settle down for a night in. But first you unlock the window. Who knows? When you're deep into Brad and *Legends of the Fall* a solvent, 6ft professional, GSOH, OHAC, NS, just might climb in…

Deal with it

Dating is essential because love hasn't climbed in a window yet. Don't approach a date as an ordeal. At worst it will be a wasted evening, at best the start of something good. Don't allow huge expectations; nothing worthwhile comes easily, unless in romantic novels. Chances are tonight won't bring you the lover of your dreams, but out of a string of such encounters something good may grow. And remember: he or she probably shares your trepidation, so put them at their ease by showing an interest in *their* life and views. Above all, don't cherish an ideal and therefore turn down anyone who doesn't, at first sight, fit the mould. Inside unprepossessing boxes magic delights may lurk.

Speed Dating
Love always speaks its name and email

HE SAYS... Speed dating is the newest and probably most bizarre method of meeting a potential partner.

You're greeted by one of two women (it's nearly always two women.) One of them is a size ten with three grand's worth of plastic boob. The other looks like the Krebs woman from Bond films. She's the muscle.

You circle a room, spending three minutes – *three minutes*: not enough time for a fruit fly to orgasm – chatting up a series of women. If you chat well she ticks your box.

Given the choice, you'd prefer most of them to leave your box alone, but you try to keep up a conversation while sliding your eyes sideways to see if anything better is coming up. It seldom is, but if it does you can tick *her* box when the time comes.

A little bell chimes when it's time to move on, usually just as you're getting up courage to ask for a phone number and sidestep the box-ticking crap. But no, you have to move on. If you don't, the muscle moves in, all thirteen stone of her.

There's not a lot you can say in three minutes.

'Hello, I'm Peter'.

'I know. I can see it on your badge.'

'Oh yes, so you can. And you're Louise. I can see it on...'

'Quite!'

Ching! Time to go.

You're sharper at the next table because this one is tasty. 'What are your interests?' she says.

'Getting out of here' springs to mind. Or 'Your bed or mine?'

Of course you don't say that. You say you're interested in politics, eating out and modern jazz. All things you hope will make you seem SUAVE. SUAVE is GOOD. It's posher than cool. (Suede used to be suave but suede jackets are more smelly than suave so beware...)

'Always identify the exit signs first.'

Anyway, being SUAVE at speed dating is essential because you have a lot to accomplish in a short time – namely to make her lust after you, which is not easy but can be done.

Sometimes you come up against a bold one who surreptitiously passes you a card with her number on.

She has to do it surreptitiously because the muscle doesn't like it.

You are *not* there to mate. You are there to circle the room unsatisfied and pay to come again.

Anyway, back to the woman who takes matters into her own hands. Men will tell you they like this, that they prefer ballsy women who know what they want.

Not strictly true.

We're flattered you made the move but wonder why you did. Are you desperate? Looking for a fall guy? Pissed? Which probably tells you more about the male psyche than anything else.

'Most women are only as good as they're painted.'

Cool women (women don't do SUAVE) make the invitation open-ended. 'We should talk more about that' is good, but necessitates your first introducing an interesting subject – and that's not easy in three minutes.

There are some guys who can cut through female defences like a hot knife through butter and generally they're not the ones you'd expect. Sometimes they're positively geeky, and you spend the next 48 hours wondering what the hell it is a woman wants in a man.

I mean, did the guy who you'd think was plankton if you saw him swimming have some secret, mysterious knowledge? If not, how come *he* knows how to make a woman drool?

You'd think women would look at a man's physique, his intellect, his salary… maybe his fingernails. If he's smart, tall and devoid of cash-flow problems he should be in.

It doesn't work that way.

The cool blonde who barely noticed your five-foot-eleven of suavity is melting over the geeky guy with tape on the left leg of his National Health spectacles. You console yourself that he's a mad scientist feeding her some unknown drug – and then you hear what he's saying.

He's discussing Uruguayan drum music.

And she's nodding like one of those dogs that dangle in a car's back window. Still, any man who can get round to Uruguayan drum music in three minutes deserves all it looks as though he's going to get.

So you try it with the next woman. (Not Uruguayan drum music: you know your own limitations, and besides which you're tone deaf.)

You go for antiques.

You do this because she has antique earrings dangling from her ear lobes. And she wears specs, which makes her look vaguely interesting.

'Do you like Byzantine art?' you say cheerfully.

She gives you a funny look, but you press on. 'Personally, I like the feel of it'. You mime a pot as you say this, just a simple hand gesture. Whether it's that or the word 'feel' - which can have lascivious overtones – she makes wild eyes at the muscle and before you know it you get your collar felt.

Net result of two hours' speed-dating: *zilch*.

You crawl home feeling low enough to walk under a duck.

And the worst thing is, it cost you twenty-five quid.

SHE SAYS... Speed dating is the IN thing. In theory it means a dazzling display of male talent will flash before your eyes until you spot Mr Right and send for a vicar.

In reality it means you have three minutes to find a nubile needle in a testosterone haystack while confronted by a terrifying treadmill of Witless Williams as desperate as you are yourself.

The first time you arrive full of hope to be greeted by a fiftyish woman with marbles in her gob and a suave thirty-something called Oliver. (He's called Oliver because almost everyone is nowadays.) He glad-hands you while marble gob takes your money and signs you up.

Emigrating can be done with less documentation but eventually Oliver leads you – or rather *flies* you, such is the force of his aftershave – to a long table filled with other female hopefuls.

'Tick my box. You'll be sorry if you don't.'

The girl on one side is chattering, but whether with fear or cold you can't be sure as she's showing more flesh than the Lido. The woman on the other side is practically salivating at the prospect of what's to come, and you get a vivid mental picture of her leaping the table to pounce on the first thing with dangly bits.

There are chairs on the opposite side of the table for the men to occupy and a pad and pen in front of you. The keen woman has been here before and shows you how you tick the box of anyone you fancy.

'Don't tick more than six,' she says. 'They don't like more than six at one session.'

You offer up a fervent prayer for at least one man who merits a tick and stow your handbag under your seat.

The three of you try to make conversation while weighing up the rest of the talent. You come to the conclusion that you're in with a chance. There are seven less attractive than you and four who leave you standing.

In what is essentially a cruel world, those aren't bad odds.

'Standing on the edge of the pool
doesn't constitute a dip...'

In the background there is music. You recognize Frank Sinatra, Johnny Mathis and a woman who sounds like Sheena Easton but could be almost anyone. They're all telling you love is in the air and the unspoken message is that soon it will be sitting opposite you.

You suddenly realize your thighs are trembling: a funny pins-and-needles kind of trembling. You clench them together in the hope it will stop – and then get a dull pain in your calf.

Only the thought that you're too young for a DVT stops you calling out for a paramedic.

You're trying to flex your leg muscles one by one when the music stops and marble gob tells you the great moment is almost here. She repeats the rules you had to read before you signed up and then the doors open and the men emerge.

'…hold your nose and plunge in!'

Oliver tries to make them sit down in orderly fashion but they are too quick for him. They all want to start with a pneumatic blonde, a Jordan-lookalike, which makes you feel indescribably bitter.

If she's so bloody attractive, what is she doing here spoiling it for the rest of you?

It seems like hours before a reluctant suitor sits down opposite you and holds out his hand.

'I'm Simon… ' he says.

His hand is dripping wet and you have to summon up all your self-control not to wipe your hand down the front of your shirt.

'I *know* you're Simon,' you say in what even you think are belligerent tones. 'I can see it on your badge.'

Simon still lives with his mother and is a Pentecostal. You remind yourself that Tom Cruise embraces a minority religion, but any other resemblance to Tom Cruise escapes you.

'It's less painful if you do it quickly.'

Still it's only three minutes, and two and three-quarters must have gone by now – but he still has time to tell you about his mother's fibromyalgia and his job as a stock analyst at a dog-food manufacturer. You pretend to tick his box because you want to send him on his way happy, but rub your hand up and down your skirt as soon as he's ensconced in the next chair.

On and on it goes.

The ones you fancy hardly seem to sit down before the buzzer goes.

You could have got pregnant and carried to full term while the ones you loathe hang in there and you go into a brown study about the passage of time until a bold one pokes you awake.

After you've binned The Lecher, The Mother's Boy, The Mute, The Boaster and The Christopher Lee Lookalike, you totter off home to lie down in a darkened room.

Such a result is not surprising.

Anyone who hopes to find anything with a pulse in three-minute bites must be daft or desperate – and that includes you.

The next morning you resolve to get a cat.

Or a dog.

Or a gerbil.

Anything with a pulse and dry palms. Animals give you unconditional love.

The way you feel right now it's either a cat or a nunnery, and you prayed for release so hard last night the latter doesn't appeal.

Deal with it

Accept that it is unlikely that the man of your dreams will appear before you, even in a group of twenty possibles. The real reward of speed dating is that it gives you experience in meeting members of the opposite sex and learning how to put them at ease – and be at ease yourself. Whether or not you get a relationship from it, speed dating will improve your ability to interact with the opposite sex. Treat each person you meet there with compassion. They, too, are hopeful and liable to be easily cast down, so do your best to boost their morale without pretending enthusiasm you don't feel. Don't keep peering ahead to see who is coming and then blank the person in front of you because you're waiting for something better. Don't try too hard to appeal or feel you must do something bizarre to make an impression within the allotted three minutes. Remember that people like talking about themselves, so be ready with questions and be prepared to answer some, too. Above all, see speed dating as a *bonus* – and not the whole purpose of life.

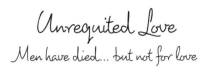

Unrequited Love
Men have died... but not for love

HE SAYS... 'I love her so much, how can she fail to love me?' is a statement which does not compute. If it did we'd all shack up with the first woman we met and miss all the fun of shopping around. Nevertheless, pressing your nose against the shop window to look at an out-of-bounds apple is not the greatest of occupations.

If you had sense you'd back off at the first put-down, but arrogance, lust, bloody-mindedness – call it what you like – keeps you hanging in there, even when she tells you her diary's full of hair-washing.

You hover at her desk, hang around the supermarket, manufacture 'accidental' meetings. If she'll let you, you become her chauffeur, gofer, dog-sitter, shelf erector and shoulder to cry on.

All this because she lets you hold her foot while you paint her toenails. Blow self respect: just being near her means you're in with a chance.

You even, abject sod that you are, drive her to dates and watch her sashay across the pavement and into *his* arms.

You let her call you 'Good old Graham' or 'Angel' even 'Chubby Chops' – all because inside you there's a cocky little voice that says she's bound to see the light eventually, because he's got red hair and a big arse and you're in shape.

And then she drops the bombshell.

St. Mark's, August 4th, and do please, *please* bring a friend. She is marrying the Overweight Ginger Whinger and you, my friend, are *history*. In vain you tell yourself the pain won't last.

Your inner voice has seen the light and says it will.

You take to drink because, sober, you see yourself going through life alone, and it sucks.

'When I love her so much how can she not love me?'

Every tramp scuttling for fag ends is you ten years from now. The single man who died at Easter and wasn't found till Christmas is your role model. For a moment you relish the prospect of being a martyr – until you realize martyrs are celibate.

Now *there's* a scary thought.

You run from it into a spate of one-night-stands, which leaves you feeling lower than before. Not only a reject but a USER!

The mood swings come then.

Anger: more fool her that she didn't see who was the better man. Humility: no wonder she turned you down – a no-hoper.

You wonder if your breath smells and breathe into your cupped hands to confirm the awful truth.

Depressed, you sit at parties sucking Amplex and gazing into a half of Carlsberg, trying to make it last the night, because if you really start drinking again where will it end?

It's a week or ten days before you begin analyzing and then it's a see-saw thing. Thoughts that you vote at opposite ends of the spectrum and you could never live in Tring, her Mecca, are rapidly superseded by regret that you didn't listen more and who would want a hallitosic no-hoper like you?

If, on the other hand, you and she *were* an item and now she's dumped you, you have two choices. You can go over and over all the times she didn't measure up, or you can wince your way through all the times you fucked up.

If you have the ability to do both, give yourself a point for balance. You're a rare man.

Most men descend into bitterness. 'She' becomes 'She-devil'. 'I did everything for that woman' becomes a mantra.

You may be different and accept that you were never in her league, but self-flagellation is a dangerous game.

So is idolatry. The moment you find yourself building a shrine around that picture of her on the back of your Harley, send for psychiatric help.

Nor should you wear your wounds in public. 'I'll come in for coffee, but it's only fair to warn you I'll never love again' is a non-starter. You know that now, but you learned it the hard way. Sod's law, nine times out of ten, the one woman you could ever love is introduced to you by your best mate: her live-in lover.

This is difficult.

In olden times you could have bested him in fair fight. Nowadays you slap him on the back and call him a lucky sod, even when he tells you the nights of passion have him knackered and God, is she a goer!

At times like that you just manage to avoid clutching your groin and keep a rictus grin firmly in place.

Phrases like 'What you've never had you never miss' are clichés invented by sadists to confuse the issue. What you've never had achieves a perfection no real romance could aspire to. Unrequited love is, by its very nature, flawless and you are landed with it. All you can do is hang in there.

All pain passes in the end and it won't kill you. Shakespeare said so. 'Men have died and worms have eaten them ... but not for love!'

The best remedy, once you're *compos mentis*, is to pen a missive to the classifieds. 'Cool, articulate male, 30ish, GSOH, N/S, into Radio Three and salsa, WLTM slim, blonde nymphomaniac with private means.'

Should I put 'cool'? No, that is SO dated. 'Quirky jazz musician seeks similar for mutual comfort...'

That should do it!

'Nature abhors a vacuum.'

SHE SAYS... Ever since Juliet wittered on about wherefore Romeo was, some woman somewhere has been looking for the man who got away.

'I loved him so much' you tell your best friend – and anyone else who will listen. The import of that remark is that love (aka grovelling devotion) should beget love.

Only it doesn't work like that.

It sometimes seems that the absence of love (aka treating men like dog-poo) produces a better result.

Which is sad but understandable, given the perversity of human nature.

Sometimes you make an enormous investment of time and effort, certain that eventually – *eventually* – he'll take off his blinkers. Bitter experience teaches you this is not the wisest move, because being a handmaiden can breed contempt.

You want to become indispensable; in fact you become wallpaper. 'My best mate' he'll call you, and *means* it.

'Heartbreak is feeling alone amidst crowds.'

He gives you affectionate hugs that produce pre-orgasmic changes in you but mean nothing to him. 'Best mates' rarely become 'bed-mates'.

You'll hand-wash his cashmere sweater, the one that matches his eyes and needs three rinses; you'll take him 'left-over casserole' that took you three hours to make.

He'll ask you round for a G&T before he takes *her* to Le Caprice.

You decide to make a graceful exit speech. 'Sod off, you ungrateful bastard' springs to mind. Instead, you smile and listen intently while he tells you her IQ's 180 and she's good with children.

He goes off to pick her up and you, who want to have his babies, go home to overdose.

Friends give you well-meaning advice to ply him with alcohol and lure him into bed. Unfortunately this means you drinking, too. You wake up six hours later and find he's covered you with a coat and gone home.

The hangover lasts three days.

Your best friend is blunt: 'Move on. There are better fish in the sea.'

This is like advising Captain Ahab to ignore the whale and settle for pilchards.

You ignore the office junior's suggestion of visiting the marvellous white witch in Hackney. If you do get him, you don't want it to be through eye of newt, much less toe of frog. Nor is it feasible to take your father's advice to wipe him from memory. As far as your pa's concerned, anyone who doesn't see his daughter's worth is a cretin. Which is probably true, but not exactly a Band-Aid for a broken heart.

You decide the cure for unrequited love is the two-pronged approach. This involves dating everything with a pulse while making detailed plans for snaring the real object of your affections. Set dates: Easter to get a night out with him, mid-summer to get him into bed, Christmas the engagement and pregnant by Twelfth Night.

Then you will vanish from his life, leaving him casserole-less and with a smelly sweater.

You'll re-appear, all sweetness and light, and fulfil his every need while giving him chapter and verse of all the dates you've been on. If there haven't been any you'll invent a few. But you'll be SUBTLE. One bunch of roses and a night at the opera is enough. You promise yourself you'll be daffy, elusive and cheerful.

Too many people think pity is akin to love; if they can provoke it they'll be home and dry. You know the man who takes pity on you doesn't see you as a sex object – he sees you as a Brownie point. When he's kind to you, it's the feel-good factor he's after, not feeling you up.

No, you need to waft in and out of his life for a while and gauge the reaction. If, by your third disappearance, he's not aggrieved (or at least curious), you'll give serious thought to hieing to a nunnery because he's not for you.

Well, you try out your strategy and it doesn't work. Furthermore he tells you proudly that he's now engaged and would you like to be his BEST WOMAN.

You go home, smash the casserole dish, tear up the dry cleaner's slip and vacuum your bra drawer. Then you book a holiday, a spa-day and a Nicky Clarke cut and style.

Numbing your pain with alcohol helps, but self-improvement is a better anaesthetic. You stop yourself giving back the key he gave you so you could water the plants. That could be seen as pique, and you must never let the enemy know you're wounded. It only feeds his ego and his is big enough.

'That which you never have you always miss.'

During the day you manage to block him out, but at night you dream about him. Everyone needs a fantasy and he is yours. But even then you know you must never, ever use him as a yardstick against which no other man could measure up.

You daydream about stitching up his pyjamas or cutting the legs from his trousers. You make yourself eat the juicy prawns rather than secrete them in his curtain pole. All those things signal that you care and take away the one thing you shouldn't be without,

DIGNITY. At least you're alive, even if you're a little bedraggled right now.

You draw out your mad money and spend it on a little pampering. Loving yourself is the greatest love of all – until someone comes along who can do it better.

Deal with it

It's tempting to imagine a world in which love would evoke love. It seldom works that way, and when it doesn't you shouldn't feel a sense of failure. If possible don't give your heart until you see some sign that it is welcome. If it's too late for caution, don't think you will never recover from the pain. Hearts are durable things, given time. Lick your wounds and try not to apportion blame. *Of course* he or she was foolish not to see your worth, but folly is not a crime. Be grateful that you have escaped a relationship in which *you* would have done all the loving – and perhaps received less than you deserve in return.

Sex
The birds and bees can keep it

HE SAYS… According to the song, birds, bees and even educated fleas do it. But they do it without *thinking*. Human beings think too much! 'How was it for you?' are the five most anxious words in the English language.

Our ability to fool ourselves over sex is limitless. If you're not getting it, you feel deprived. Even your parents had it at least once – *you* are the only being in the universe without a lay.

You fantasize about it and, boy, are you GOOD in imagination and, boy, is she GRATEFUL!

On the odd occasion you do it for real, she's more likely to reach for a nail-file and say 'Are you done yet?' but you manage to blot out such painful memories.

So there you are, nose pressed to the glass and life going on the other side. The theory is that you can always get sex of a sort – and we're *not* talking paying for it. Be kind to a woman in need of positive feedback and you're in, they say. If she's worried that she's past her prime, she's grateful but if she even hints at the biological clock words, scarper. You might get more than you bargain for.

And beware of women whose bodies are temples, open to all and sundry. Welcoming they may be; safe they're not.

The trouble is that if you accept sex as a release and not a romantic thing you're liable to wind up with a little knot of something inside you – hurt or self-disgust, I don't know – that refuses to go away.

Women think we'll leap on anything and crow about it afterwards. True for some, but not for all. If you refuse to take the easy-come-easy-go road, you console yourself with the thought that masturbation is genetically inherited behaviour passed on by our primeval forefathers.

In other words, it's not our fault.

(I don't know which geneticist discovered that but he should be canonized.)

Live in a sex-free wasteland for a while and you worry. Will you ever again get the chance to do it? Will you rise to the occasion if you do? Is it true that a big nose equals a big pecker (in which case you're sunk)? Is it true that bald men are extra-virile, and if so would tearing out your hair help? Are Caucasian penises smaller than almost any others, especially African Americans? (Those damn Yanks again!)

Most of the myths are as true as condoms being good for baby-making, but in the wee small hours you're a sucker for tall tales.

During the day you are constantly tantalized, because men are visual beings where sex is concerned. While Einstein was discovering relativity a sliver of cleavage, a flash of thigh could put him right off. If he hadn't battled on, he might never have found his Theory.

Today, with women putting everything in the shop window, a man's groin is activated hourly – which is why we haven't discovered anything much since the bagless vacuum cleaner.

'If a body meet a body lying in the rye, you can be sure crops will be the last thing on their minds.'

Even when you enter into a steady sexual relationship, anxiety continues. Just before you're about to unveil the mystery of the universe to your new woman, she tells you that her ex was a bastard but a lion in the sack.

No pressure then, no pressure!

You also find she has an agenda that resembles final exams. You've just mastered the missionary position and she wants your leg round your neck. When she produces the furry bondage gear you cut and run.

You saw that Kathy Bates film – no one's tying *you* to a bed.

Next time you pick someone a little more demure. By now you've learned that the way to get a woman into bed is to let her talk non-stop. All you have to do is chuck in the odd 'Of course' and 'You know I do' and she's happy.

'Go on, surprise me!'

You've also read every sex book ever written, two of them with diagrams.

The trouble is that when you begin to make love to her, this talking machine shuts up, just when you could do with a little encouragement. 'I love that incredible thing you're doing' would do.

Instead she says 'Did we turn the cooker off?'

Hasn't she *heard* about windows of opportunity!?

On the average, a man gets seven erections a day but most of them are in his sleep, and she's just wasted one of the daytime ones sending you downstairs to check the gas.

Suppose you're in a good relationship. Sex is regular, satisfying and mutually appreciated. You're doing it at least twice a week – and then someone in the pub talks about seven times a night and twice while dinner cooks and you're back where you started: insecure.

How come lechers have all the fun?

One day you realize that what you have is the best you'll ever get. For a moment there's a twinge of regret that there'll be no more hunting, and then you sigh a contented sigh and settle back. In the sex manuals it says this period - the infatuation period - doesn't last, next comes something called 'the attachment stage' and nooky dwindles, presumably because you're busy putting up shelves.

But hell: what do textbooks know?

SHE SAYS... It pains me to say it, but sex is a chemical thing. Forget brain or eye; forget intellectual stimulation or aesthetic appreciation. If a guy smells right, that's it.

You can read about it in pharmaceutical journals: it's all down to dopamine, the brain's natural feel-good chemical. So all that stuff you're fed in school –

Shakespeare and Lochinvar and knights fighting dragons for love of a lady – is so much *bunk*.

Nor is it a man's six-pack, or his soulful eyes, it's his *dopamine*.

Sordid, isn't it? One day you'll just take a pill and have an orgasm and not a man in sight.

At the moment, though, we're stuck with the old model – which is a depressing enough thought.

The one thing men seem to miss is that women need to feel *valued* before they can give and receive good sex. Driving you to his place or yours does *not* count as foreplay.

Women need to be WOOED.

Praise her, stroke her, play her wall-to-wall Barry White and her libido stretches and gets out of bed.

What does *not* impress her is being phoned after three month's silence by a guy who says 'I've been thinking about you all night'. Translated, that means he hasn't had sex for six weeks and his book fell open at your page.

Or, worse still, he's been through the other pages and you're his last hope.

Even when you make it to the bed there's a yawning gulf between male and female expectations. He wants a swift coupling and then a sound sleep. You want INTIMACY. You want to lie entwined, sharing secrets and giggles, putting off the moment when anything mechanical happens.

For you it could all happen in the mind (well, most of it).

He wants to switch on the motor and thinks your nipples are on/off and volume.

Would that it were that simple.

'Give a man a free hand and guess where he'll put it?'

And if you don't turn on and whirr for him, he suggests you're wanting in some way. He may even suggest you 'see someone' – although if *he's* the one with the problem, he'd rather cut off his testicles with a blunt instrument than 'see' anybody.

If he's the determined type and you don't want to play, he'll make a move for what he erroneously considers to be your erogenous zones. The one organ he'll ignore is your brain, although it's the biggest sexual muscle of them all. So he'll fumble with your bra or your knee and entirely miss the need to whisper in your ear.

(OK, he's got a couple of million sperms to deal with, but that's why God gave him a brain and self-control, so why does he try to put the problem in *your* lap?)

In the end he's such a nuisance that you fake it just to get it over and that is NOT satisfactory.

That's why so many women are seeking other outlets: a giggle with the girls at an Ann Summers party, a night at a club watching *men* slither round poles for a change, a pamper session at a spa with not a hairy chest in sight.

'If God had wanted you to think with your genitalia would he have bothered to give you a brain?'

At least the average sex maniac is understandable.

More difficult are the oddballs who idealize women: Madonna fags. They can't accept that we get horny, too.

The Victorians believed that women were asexual. They'd lie back and think of England in return for a bed and three square meals a day but they never *wanted* it. And the odd woman who did want it was a whore and not acceptable in polite circles. That's why Queen Victoria had to keep quiet about being a right little raver. Poor Albert died young, quite worn out! (She said as much in her diary.)

The truth is that we're every bit as lustful as men, it just takes a different and more complicated combination to open the safe.

That old regime was very comforting for men. No obligation to tease or please as long as you got it over quickly to allow the lady-wife to turn over and slumber. As for your mistress or the serving wench, she was at your beck and call.

Nowadays men have the big 'O' hanging over them. Can they, will they, have they brought you to orgasm? And if they have, was it ten decibels above what you got from the last guy?

No wonder they feel threatened!

They also make major mistakes about what turns a woman on. What's this male obsession with the waxed torso? A tantalizing glimpse of chest hair, a fuzzy darkness below the waist and we clean forget what we intended to cook for dinner so why do they sidle into salons and bite towels as the wax is ripped off?

As for thongs, I'd sooner watch paint dry than a prat in a posing pouch pretending he's looking for his trousers so he can give you an all round view.

The other big turn-off is guys who have names for their willies. 'Rupert is up for it tonight' is enough to send a thinking female screaming into the woods.

Another no-no is being asked the daftest place you've done it. On the roof of the *Orient Express*? In a broom cupboard? On a pool table in the Lochaber Hilton? What's special about *discomfort*?

Such questions are irritating.

So is the male obsession with knowing how many previous partners you've had. If he thought about it, he could work it out (well, roughly). One every three months, four a year, ten years: twenty – well, actually it's a bit less than that and none of his business. But no, he wants you to *say* it for him and he'd like the answer to be three and he's the best by far.

Because, deep down, today's man is *scared*. He's no longer on top and it shows.

'Life is a sexually transmitted disease.'

Which is sad because, deep down, today's woman still wants roses round the door and happy-ever-after with a strong man. She may pay the mortgage, she may rod the drains, but in bed she wants wonderful, fulfilling sex – emotion in motion, as Mae West called it.

When she realizes that at last she's got it – and it may take years – she feels overwhelming relief.

Deal with it

Used properly, sex enhances life. Misused or treated carelessly, it can create havoc. Embrace it, don't fear it; take the trouble to thoroughly understand it. It's amazing how many people have only a rudimentary understanding of their own bodies and sexuality. Sex is powerful – but don't see it as a panacea for all woes, or the glue that can hold a disintegrating relationship together. Wonderful as it is, it should always be the icing on the cake – *not* the cake itself.

Food
There's no such thing as a little bit of garlic

HE SAYS… Relationships are a lot like food. You marry a blonde and spend the rest of your life salivating over brunettes, just as you order liver and then watch every morsel of your companion's osso bucco from plate to mouth.

Food can be an important indicator of the state of a relationship. It can also be a warning light. If, on a first date, she tells you her tortellini is to die for and she only lives to make puff pastry, she sees herself in the kitchen, baby in the high-chair, toddler in the garden, you in the office forty pounds overweight, slaving to pay for it all.

Unless you, too, are broody run like hell.

If, on the other hand, she is keen to dissociate herself from things domestic she's probably a ball-breaker. If she snatches the Wine List and tells the sommelier to bring château-bottled '92 grown on the north side of the vineyard and can he close that window while he's at it, you're in the hands of a control freak.

You sweat through the meal reconsidering your plan to split the bill. But if you pay there are two problems: will your card stretch to château-bottled and will she then feel obliged to see you again, a consummation devoutly to be unwished?

On the other hand, if you let her pay (and she'll probably insist) a life of servitude could beckon. This fear is confirmed when she tells you what to eat and orders it for you. While she divides her plate into sections – carbohydrates, protein, fibre and E numbers – you consider going to the loo and ringing for reinforcements.

That's when you remember you're a MAN.

'A little sauce goes a long way.'

You get out your card between main course and dessert and keep feeling it in your pocket. It is your shield and buckler. Once it's swiped, you're free. You make your excuses before coffee and while ostensibly at the loo, pay the bill.

Just remember not to sit through coffee with a grin of relief on your face. It might be misinterpreted.

If you're lucky, you'll be sharing that meal with a foodie. She obviously likes eating (her cleavage is ample). You hope she'll order something gooey which will drip down that fascinating cleft, allowing you to wipe it away. She oohs and aahs at her own food and licks her lips at yours. You offer her tempting titbits on a fork and she takes them between dainty teeth.

This lady knows how to enjoy the good things in life. She leaves the wine to you, offers to go halves with the bill, doesn't make a scene when you say no and invites you back for coffee.

This one you like, but don't go overboard before you've inspected her pad. It could tell you a lot.

If she has thirty-one different spices in a rack, all turned to face the same way, she probably has obsessive-compulsive disorder. A clinical kitchen denotes a mean spirit; a pristine bedroom likewise. However ample she is, a Cruella De Vil could lurk beneath.

'Life is too short for fish knives and forks.'

Check her magazine rack. Any bridal magazine is a red alert unless she's already told you her best friend/sister is getting married. If you get the chance, press her pedal bin. Its contents might surprise you. There may also be empty bottles stashed behind it. A bad sign.

Somewhere along the line, if everything has gone well and she's cooked for you, you'll invite her back to your place. You know her tastes by now: artistic starter, main course not too spicy but succulent, a creamy pud and a nice bit of cheese to end with. (There's something about a woman who appreciates the importance of cheese and knows it takes more than plain water biscuits to bring out the flavour…)

Don't try to compete. Display flair and you weaken your chances of a life where you only have to open your beak at feeding times to have it filled with a tempting morsel.

It's OK to buy precooked meals. Too much marinating and she might think you're gay. If you've already disabused her of that idea, it's OK to dress the salad.

If possible, avoid shopping together. Your method of slinging things into the trolley or scooping up half-price rejects you don't like (but can't resist) won't do. She will have a LIST and a beady eye for use-bys.

For years you've scraped the mould off jam or fish paste and never ailed a thing. Don't tell her this or her scream will stop the shoppers in thirteen aisles.

If you're in a long-term relationship, remember not to use the word 'anything' when she asks you what you want for supper. In the first flush of romance, you say 'anything' and she goes off to produce culinary gems.

Once out of the honeymoon period say 'Oh, anything' and she may well batter you with her fists and accuse you of putting all the responsibility onto *her*. She misses her mother, her boss hates her and she wishes she was dead.

Another no-no answer is 'What have you got?' This will get you a list of pantry contents encompassing stock cubes, tinned soup and rich tea fingers. Then she'll tell you she wants her mother, she wishes you were dead and why do you put everything onto *her*?

On the other hand, if you tell her precisely what you want, she'll probably burst into tears because she's got in everything but the thing you chose. She's failed you, which is all *your* fault, she misses her mother and she wishes she was dead.

Which all boils down to the fact that you can't win.

Just smile winsomely and tell her whatever she cooks will be wonderful. That does it every time!

'Slaving over a hot stove makes for cold sex.'

SHE SAYS… From agonizing over who pays the bill to wondering whether or not you should offer breakfast to a one-night stand, food is a minefield. Even in these enlightened times, don't believe its provision is anything other than a female province.

OK, once in a while he says he'll cook, you put your feet up and enjoy a G&T – but not until *you've* shopped for the ingredients, cleaned the veg (unless you want to be eating grit all night), laid all the right utensils and seasonings where even he can't miss them and set the table. Afterwards the kitchen will look like an abandoned campsite and you'll never again find your best knife: the one with the thin blade and the point that would get in anywhere, especially between his ribs.

Of course there are some suave individuals who will invite you to their pad and do the cordon bleu bit.

Be careful.

If the first course is oysters and the main course sweetbreads, make a run for it. *You* are dessert.

Be similarly wary of any man who buys you Turkish Delight in bulk, especially if he tells you it's Turkish name is *Rahat Lokum* (pronounced 'Lakooom'). Make your excuses and leave because he has a vision of you lying on a silk couch stuffing your face with *Rahat Lokum* while waiting for his sultan to devour you. You are a goose being stuffed for foie gras, and it's not a pleasant feeling.

You can learn a lot about men from their choice of

food. If they're picky, they're probably mean. Not that being a voracious eater necessarily hides a giving spirit; if he really likes his grub he'll expect you to provide it round the clock.

There are better things to do with your life.

Most men have a weakness for 'nursery' food, even those who didn't have a nanny or a Peter Rabbit plate. Nursery food is comfort food: soft, warm and apparently predigested. If he wheedles you to make him soldiers with his boiled egg, be alarmed. If it's sticky toffee pudding with custard *and* cream, join a dating agency. Such a man is NEEDY. If you don't want a life of servitude, move on.

Not all men are foodies, and on a first date you shouldn't necessarily look for bad signs. You have other things to contend with – like who pays! How I wish I could give you a definitive answer to that question but it remains a riddle hidden in an enigma. Broadly speaking, the person who issues the invitation should pay, but today's woman likes to show she's willing. 'Here, let me' is enough, but make a gesture towards your handbag if you want the offer to sound authentic.

If the evening has gone well, he hasn't asked for oysters or sticky toffee pudding or squeezed your knee under the cloth, you can accept gracefully and say 'Next time's on me'. You want to see him again. If, on the other hand, he accepts your offer and says next time's on him, beware. His idea of next time may be two hot dogs and a six-pack at a drive-in.

If he has exhibited revolting table habits or shown a marked disinterest in what will happen to you after he's eaten your share of the chocolates, that response won't do. Instead, say 'It's very good of you' or, if you have a Calvinist conscience, INSIST on going Dutch. Use the latter if his eyes bulged when he saw the bill or he's feverishly searching his pockets for change.

Whatever happens about the bill, put it behind you. No need to go to confession because you let down your sex. No need to feel a cheat because you went straight home instead of paying in kind. No point in wishing you'd ordered the pot roast at £6.99 instead of the Duck à la Grecque at £21.50. *He* asked you out, he had your company and he's probably charging it to expenses anyway. And if you paid and he let you, he's either too New a man or a cheapskate. Write it off to experience.

At any time one of you may be on a diet. If he's trying to make the weigh-in for amateur steeple-chasing, don't make him watch *The Food Programme*. If it's you who is dieting, don't expect him to share your plain boiled cabbage. Nor should you give him a piled plate of fry-up and serve yourself shredded fennel.

Sharing a meal is meant to be a *joy*, not a guilt trip.

How's this for a scary scenario? He's taken you to three expensive restaurants and refused all offers to split the bill. You can't afford to reciprocate in the same style. You must invite him to your place. The snag is you can only cook plain boiled spaghetti with melted cheese triangles and black pepper garnish.

'The way to a man's heart is through the delicatessen.'

Three options here. Let him know the brutal truth: that kitchens are not your scene. Patronize the local deli and put the cartons down the waste disposal well before he arrives, reasoning that your culinary ineptitude is best kept secret until you have become sexually indispensable. Or thirdly, take a crash course in nouvelle cuisine and remember the golden rule: meals for men need only contain meat and beer. (NB Whichever course you take, remember never to serve gas-producing foods within two hours of bedtime).

When the time comes for you to visit his place, remember that anything he has prepared, no matter how awful, should be masticated slowly between yelps of delight. His ego requires no less. Accept that men were born to poke the campfire, not to stir the pot. In time we can change that but not overnight.

Halfway through the preparation he'll probably scream that he's cut off his finger. Your natural inclination will be to turn off the pans. Resist it. He will think you callous. Instead, gently remove the tea towel he's clutching to the wound and try to find the blood he can't bear to look at but wants you to stem. Coo softly while doing this then send him off to nurse his bad arm while you dish up. Resist the impulse to throw everything out and start again. A man has his pride.

At table, extricate the burned bits from your mouth unobtrusively and slip them into your pocket. If no pocket is present, your bra will do, but remember to retrieve them before adjourning for afters.

The way to a man's heart is no longer through his stomach. Nor, contrary to common belief, is it situated twelve inches below that organ. It lies in his EGO, that tiny, intangible thing which governs his every move. Bruise it at your peril.

Deal with it

For some people, food is an aphrodisiac. For others, eating is a chore, the pursuit of something to eat a waste of time. Let the one with flair provide the food, the other do the chores. When possible, give food it's proper setting: soft lights, sweet music and, above all, *time*. The demands of modern living don't always allow this, but whenever you can, make the effort. Don't despise shortcuts like the microwave or takeaway, but if they become the norm you are missing out. Food can be helpful at times of stress, but never see it solely as a comforter. Treat it with respect and it will serve you well.

Parties
I should have stayed at home

HE SAYS... The one unshakeable truth about parties is that the ones you look forward to are turkeys and the ones you're dragged to are sometimes fruitful.

We all know how it is in the movies: you enter a room, take a drink from a flunkey, look up and meet the eyes of your soul mate. Half an hour later you make your excuses and leave together, to live happily ever after.

Real life is different to movies.

In real life parties fall into two categories: private and grand. Believe me, they're different! For the private party, there's the BYOB dilemma. You buy a bottle then decide it isn't good enough, go back and buy another. By the fourth bottle you have something so expensive it merits Securicor and you're worried they'll think you're a pretentious git.

Then there's the obstacle that is called 'getting ready' (this pertains to both varieties). For ten minutes you try to decide whether or not to squeeze the dome-sized zit that has appeared on or about your nose. You settle for a facial scrub, hot water, soft bristles. Then you apply foam or shaving oil and shave. That does for the zit, but now you look like an accident victim.

You bathe or shower, use shampoo and conditioner, apply deodorant and then gel or wax your hair. You put in your contacts and flinch at what the mirror reveals. Moisturizer and cologne help a little, then you put your clothes on, aware that you're now sweating so profusely that the last forty minutes have been wasted time.

By the time you reach the party your only hope is that you'll be electrocuted by the doorbell. You're about to ring when you look at your watch: 7.25 and the invite was for 7.30. You retreat to an opposite doorway because you haven't the bottle to be the first to arrive.

You wait till you see other people arriving. They're all strangers to you, but greet one another with whoops of joy. So that's how it's going to be: CLIQUEY.

You ponder going home but that's defeatist, so you pin your hopes on the doorbell, but (Sod's Law) it's fully earthed. You knock and enter.

None of the 470 people you know are there.

This party is peopled by ALIENS.

You put your bottle among all the others, accept a drink that smells like cider vinegar and look for somewhere to skulk. It's 7.40 and you can't leave before 9 o'clock – 8.45 tops.

The night stretches before you like a spell in the nick. All around you people are getting on like streets on fire. Some of them even pair up and vanish. You feel a frisson of disapproval before envy kicks in.

'If you've seen one party you've seen 'em all.'

Why couldn't that have been *you*? It's the last straw.

You finish up your cider vinegar and slink away, but not before finding your hostess. You don't want to do this but you were well brought up and your mother can see through walls.

'Lovely party, wouldn't have missed it but the dog's got the runs. Can't be left… '

She doesn't remember you haven't got a dog because she seems to have forgotten who you are. She goes *Mwah* on your left cheek and then *Mwah* on your right and her eyes shift back to her other guests.

Walking home you promise yourself never, *ever* to accept another invitation, all the while knowing that optimism always triumphs.

You'll do it next month. With a bit of luck it might even be next week.

Grand parties are held in function rooms and are usually associated with WORK. You love your job. You're good at it, but when it comes to social gatherings confidence oozes away as you shower. You think of all the *faux pas* you might commit and it's a buttock-clenching thought.

Other people don't seem to have a problem. They move from one to another, smiling, tinkling, saying just enough and moving on.

You realize you're watching social intercourse. You've often wondered what that meant.

Now you know.

You shrink back into your corner feeling socially inferior, completely forgetting you were Performer of the Year in the staff magazine. Here you're a social reject.

You go on feeling inferior until your fifth glass of wine and then you think to hell with it: if mixing is the name of the game, you can mix with the best of them.

The first woman you accost has a fixed smile and eyes that wander left and right, looking for someone more important than you. It doesn't take long. She says 'Excuse me' and moves on.

You're about to scuttle back into your corner when you see someone else has occupied it. She looks desperate –

more desperate than *you*. Two desperates don't make a valiant. You move to the buffet and pile a plate.

You want a wall to lean against but there isn't a spare inch. You move through the crowd to the centre of the room, trying to balance your drink and your plate in one hand while taking food to your mouth with the other.

That's when you realize your eyes were bigger than your belly. Two bites of a drumstick and you're not only full, you're *gagging*. You move the chicken right to left in your mouth and realize it's mostly gristle. You try to remove it – and that's when your drink tips down your shirt. Mortified, you look around but no one is taking any notice.

You're relieved.

You're also pissed off.

You could have a heart attack in the middle of this lot and they wouldn't stop yakking long enough to give you mouth-to-mouth.

As you make your way back to the buffet to dump the plate, you have to charge solid walls of Armani tailoring on guys called Philip or Jakey or Tom. They all have loud, confident voices and they're having a GOOD time.

You try very hard to despise them, but it doesn't work. You contemplate spilling your plate down a sharp-suited back but they all have women clinging to them – women in floaty chiffon who are regarding you with deep suspicion.

You clutch the plate even harder and say sorry, sorry, sorry all the way across to the buffet.

Mission accomplished. You breathe again.

Now you can go home and – sod that! It's not yet eight o'clock and the MD might notice you're not there. (The MD doesn't realize you exist, fat chance of him missing you in this lot.)

That's when you notice the girl who got your corner. She's watching you and there's a little smile – well, what *looks* like a smile, hovering round her lips.

They're nice lips. Quite full but not noticeably surgically enhanced, which is rare nowadays when a man has to watch what he touches in case it bursts.

You smile, she smiles back. If she wasn't on the other side of all the suits and chiffon… and then you notice she's holding a mobile phone. You get your phone out and raise it aloft. She frowns and you start holding up fingers. One, two, three four… suddenly she nods and makes an 0 with thumb and finger. You punch it in and she gives you seven fingers and seven again. You go on keying in numbers then you text her.

'YR we at this ASI9 pty?'

She grins and shrugs and you text 'Outside?'.

She nods again and puts her phone back in her bag.

Outside it's windy and you shelter in a doorway until she comes out. At close quarters she looks like Sandra Bullock. You've always fancied Sandra Bullock. 'I know a pub' you say and take her elbow to dodge the traffic.

She says 'Lovely party' and you say 'Yes' because, actually, it wasn't too bad after all.

SHE SAYS... It's been in your diary for ages and you're well-prepared. You've enquired about the dress code and it's 'something casual' which means your M&S flowered gypsy skirt, black GAP top, big silver earrings and your black wedges.

You exfoliate, depilate, shave your legs and floss your teeth, then get a shower, blow-dry your hair and paint your toenails.

So far so good.

You drink a glass of milk to put a lining on your stomach, but you don't eat anything solid because there's sure to be a buffet and you're not sure you can fasten the top of your skirt.

You take ages over your make-up, blending the base right down your neck and into your hairline like they do in magazines. Concealer, powder, blusher, eyeliner, two shadows (light and dark), and then lipliner.

You look like a clown, so you scrub with tissue which brings blood to the surface of your skin and you look *worse*. Like Pocahontas, in fact.

You powder feverishly then do your lips. If the lights are low, you'll get away with it.

You put on the flowered skirt and the black top and they look crap together so you take the top off and try another one.

It sucks.

Five tops later you bin the flowered skirt and all the tops and start working down from the earrings. An hour later, you're wearing your old navy suit, but the earrings look good.

You decide to spring for a taxi, but while you wait for it you give serious consideration to not going. You hardly know the people whose party it is, everyone there will be married or spoken for and the only people who will speak to you will be intellectual snobs. ('What do you do?' 'I'm an admin. assistant.' 'How interesting. Excuse me, there's someone over there I must speak to…')

You wonder what would happen if you'd said you were Richard Branson's PA or next in line to be a high court judge, but sod it: why *should* you lie?

In the end you get in the taxi and rehearse the excuses you'll make when you leave early. You dismiss saying your waters have broken because they know you're not pregnant, and anyway they might call an ambulance. Nor can you say you have another party to go to because that's pretentious.

In the end you realize that you can just melt away and no one will notice – you're not important enough to be missed. Which is a bummer, but gives you enough courage to get through the door.

The hostess is engaged in animated conversation with someone who looks vaguely familiar, from telly or something. Her husband says, 'So glad you could come,' while looking over your shoulder for the next arrival. He shoves a drink in your hand and says, 'Do mix.'

You move forward between women in floaty dresses showing acres of flesh. Your navy suit covers you from chin to knee. If backs bare to the bumcrack are 'something casual', it's news to you.

You give serious thought to telling everyone you thought it was fancy dress so you came as a Health Visitor but decide against it. Maybe you can do a chameleon and meld with the wallpaper, which is shades of navy and charcoal and must have cost the earth.

In front of you is a woman in a scarlet dress slashed to the thigh. It's a fuck-me dress and, judging from the crowd of men around her, that could be a self-fulfilling prophecy. She has fabulous hair: carrot-red and abundant enough for her to keep flicking it back. You hate her with a passion, especially when you realize she is pale gold and smooth all over.

'Don't drink if you want to know you're having a good time.'

Why are *you* the only woman in the world with wrinkled elbows? For the first time that evening you're glad you came well-wrapped up (some things are better left unseen).

Not for the first time you search for the reason why you're so bad at private parties. At official functions you sparkle, never pushing but making sure the top brass know you're there. You feel confident when it comes to work.

When it comes to being a WOMAN, a human being among other human beings, you feel like crap. Observation reveals that every woman in the room is teetering on strappy Jimmy Choo three-inch heels.

Every woman but *you*. You have navy-blue shoes with heels and toes and sturdy, one-inch heels.

Embarrassment gets you moving. If you move fast enough, no one will notice your feet. You fix a smile on your face, hold your glass aloft and press on.

On the fourth circuit of the room you've run out of 'Scuse me's' and look for a seat. Besides, your feet are killing you, which isn't fair because the Jimmy Choos are doing fine, not a torn Achilles tendon in sight.

The seats have all been removed so the room can be packed like sardines. You move to the side, lean against the wall, take one foot out and rub it against your other ankle.

Bliss.

For the first time you wonder if you might just stick this one out. There's a tall man filling his plate at the buffet. He's a bit untidy and you find that endearing. He's also hungry because he piles his plate up like someone stacking Lego. When he can't add another olive he moves from the table and tries to juggle plate and glass. Eventually he lifts the plate to his mouth and takes a *vol au vent* from it with his teeth.

It makes you laugh and you look around, terrified anyone heard you. Only loonies laugh when they're on their own. To laugh properly, you need friends, an audience, someone to tell you a joke. You contemplate doing a PhD in laughter; the research would be fun…

Then you notice that the plate man has spilled wine down his shirt. His lips make a word and it isn't 'Spit'.

You resist the desire to go over and offer your hanky. Instead, you take out your phone to ring for a taxi. At home there's half a bottle of Pinot Grigio in the 'fridge, you can put on your fluffy dressing gown, put the navy suit in the Oxfam bag and watch that old black-and-white movie you taped at the weekend.

You're about to dial the number when the plate-filler looms. 'Could you do me a huge favour?' he says, thrusting his plate at you. Suddenly you have a mission: you're a healer, not a hanger-on.

You hold his plate, offer a tissue and generally make him feel less like a social incompetent than he did a minute ago. You're getting ready to have his babies when a pair of Jimmy Choos stroll up.

'Darling,' she says, 'you'll have to wash that shirt yourself. I *did* warn you.'

He looks at you apologetically and just for a moment his eyes tell you he's thinking babies, too. And then he's gone.

You slip outside and run till you reach the main road. There's a taxi coming and in a moment you're safe inside and speeding home. Tomorrow you'll send your hostess flowers and a card saying 'Lovely party'. That way you might get asked again.

Deal with it

Enjoy yourself at office parties, but not so much that you can't face work the next morning. Other parties may eventually seem a drag. You have such hopes for them – hopes that are almost never realized. But the exciting thing about parties is that each one has a dynamic of its own. The next one, the one you almost skip, may be the night of your dreams. At worst, it's one wasted night out of a lifetime. So top up your glass, sit back, and if you do nothing else, watch the pantomime of human nature at play.

Bad Behaviour

Chivalry isn't dead, it's in a permanent vegetative state

HE SAYS... Once upon a time women behaved impeccably. If they didn't, they were classed as 'easy' or worse still, 'common'. Definitely not to be taken home to mother.

Nowadays the female of the species is hell-bent on copying male characteristics, but only the worst ones. I mean, we don't *all* get legless and lie in gutters shrieking 'Barcelona', but they think that's the initiation to the club.

Women think they're superior to men, and in one way they are: when they decide to do something, they do it WHOLEHEARTEDLY. Where a man might get tipsy, a woman will announce her intention to get 'bladdered', and weave along the pavement arm-in-arm with her mates until she's succeeded.

The latest aim seems to be to get arrested for knocking a policeman's hat off. That used to be *our* privilege on cup final nights.

Equality? They won't be happy till they've taken *everything*. When men drink, they get chummy – they love everyone. Either that or they go silent.

Women get aggressive or talkative. Booze makes

them bold. Get a few vodka martinis down and she'll phone Barclay's and ask them to wipe out her overdraft ('You did it for Africa, you can do it for me!').

Drink also makes them randy. No matter what they say, forget the idea that women have abandoned that old dream of babies and roses round the door. What is Bridget Jones waiting for? It isn't Godot; it's a MAN.

'I'm not so think as you drunk I am.'

The difference is that now they don't really want you in the background. They want a Giro from the Child Support Agency with your hard-earned money behind it. Any woman (unless she's your nan) has a biological clock set at five to midnight. If you get the whiff of a tick, run like hell.

When women were sweet, pretty things hanging on our every word (I mean, watch a Merchant Ivory film), we didn't mind them being a bit feather-headed. Now they rule the world, but they're still inconsistent.

Men have a sense of proportion. Women don't. The woman who hoards 2p coupons for products she seldom buys will splash out £500 on a handbag notable only for a 'G' or a 'P' on the logo.

The greatest inconsistency of all is their attitude to *sex*! They run home to mother if their man pauses under the mistletoe at Christmas while happily bed-hopping themselves.

This is NEW.

'Disgust is jealousy hiding behind a halo.'

Women have often betrayed men, but they kept it quiet because they were ashamed of it. Men might boast, but women had more grace. Now they'll happily tell the tabloids how many lays they've had this week. Scarlet woman rules!

When it comes to sex women have not only caught up with men, they've out-classed them. They are bolder, coarser and keener to state their requirements. The last woman to lie back and think of England was Margaret Thatcher, and she was coming from a different viewpoint.

Nowadays it's women who yell 'Get 'em off as male strippers gyrate. Men sit impassive before lapdancers. You may drool a bit, but you keep your hands clenched (or in your pocket). Women grab and guess what's most available.

The tabloids call such women *ladettes*.

Have you *looked* at them? 'Navviettes' would be nearer the mark. They seem to have cast off caution.

Once they dabbed their eyes in rows. Now they throw things – and this is where it gets *really* despicable. When you get tired of ducking and make for the door, ten to one they plead 'time of the month'. You had a mother and three sisters and you don't remember them baying every time the moon was full.

Mind you, when she isn't addled, today's woman can be great. She isn't after a meal ticket because she earns her own; she comes straight to the point, lets you know when the sex was good and thumps you when it wasn't so that you know where you stand.

Oh, and headaches are a thing of the past. If you find a woman like that, grab her.

SHE SAYS... Male bad behaviour? How long have you got? Sometimes it seems they make a life's work out of swearing, farting, mooning and making cheap sexist jokes, all the while drowning in a sea of lager!

And that's just the weekends.

But what really irritates the hell out of women is men's belief – no, *conviction* – that one little word, five little letters, will expunge the whole episode of mayhem from your feeble female brain.

Here's news for you, boys.

The female brain would baffle Bill Gates. There's a compartment for everything and you're in there, baby. BIG TIME. Right down to the lager stain on my one bit of Nicole Farhi that cost thirteen quid to clean.

They use the 'sorry' word when they've been unfaithful. 'Sorry', they say, trying hard to look like Hugh Grant: all Little Boy Lost and floppy-haired. 'I'm really sorry. It didn't mean anything.'

More news for you, baby. It means 'You're outta here'.

You've got to get rid. If you don't, they'll still be saying it was 'meaningless' when the bill for child support comes in.

Then there's manners. Once upon a time a man walked on the outside of the pavement so you didn't get splashed. Nowadays he sends you to get the car in case his hair gets wet. Chivalry is not only dead, it's cremated and the ashes scattered.

Before you point it out, I admit there have always

been men who were boorish or drunken or downright objectionable. But they were OUTCASTS. Now they're *all* at it so there's nowhere to banish anyone to.

Loutishness has been elevated to an art form. Drink's to blame for a lot of it. You hope he'll remember the anniversary of the day you met? Honey, he can't remember last night! He couldn't make it to the bed and there's a mark across his cheek where he lay for five hours with his face in the dog's bowl.

'You don't have to make a monkey of a man.
He does it for himself.'

You make a lasagne verde for a special occasion. He's 'just having one with the guys from the office'. The 'one' lasts so long that the lasagne is burned to a crisp, he spends an hour in the bathroom throwing up and then you have to stuff an apple in his mouth to stop him calling you 'pet', and swearing undying love. A gallon of coffee later he sits like Buddha intoning 'Never again' and you realize that MAN really is the missing link between the ape and civilization.

Part of the trouble is that the sexes mature at different rates. A girl of seventeen is a WOMAN. A youth of seventeen has knuckles that trail the floor, rampant acne and spends his time arm-wrestling his best mate.

Not that the mature version is much improvement.

Adult males are either competent liars or have lost their grip on reality. Evidence? 'I did not have sex with that woman' should do. You can be the most powerful man on the planet and still be a fantasist.

A woman wouldn't have done it in the first place.

If she had, she'd have held her hands up as soon as she was rumbled.

'And the pig got up and slowly walked away.'

Most women can put up with boorishness, meanness even, the odd spot of chatting up a posh frock, but all of us draw the line at schoolboy antics. Take mooning. Footballers on sixty grand a week will drop their trousers for fun. Some men do it in taxi windows and it's not a pretty sight.

And the puerile jokes! 'Whooah! Look at the melons on her' is COARSE, even when it falls from the lips of an old Etonian.

Men seldom behave like this except when part of

the pack – and therein lies the problem. Men are pack animals and when in packs they run amok. Even singly they can make you cringe, clicking their fingers for service, talking to your cleavage; they even do that in the office, mistaking your knee for dough that wants kneading.

All men are closet bread-makers.

The sad fact is that men in the main are coarse creatures. No wonder so many female scientists are working on a substitute.

Deal with it

The purpose of good manners is to make life pleasant for everyone. If your desire to 'be yourself' or to prick pomposity makes others uncomfortable, where's the sense in doing it? Genuine irreverence and spontaneous clowning have their place, but beware of becoming 'the class clown'. Such people are not seen as daring for long. They become a bore and an embarrassment.

Work
All play and no work makes for big trouble

HE SAYS… Fraternization is not encouraged in your workplace. In fact, it's almost *verboten* – but hope springs eternal.

You set your alarm that little bit earlier so you can shower, always wear a clean shirt, use mouthwash and generally present a spruce appearance. And can you pull? Not a nibble, except for dotty Dora in Subsidiary Accounts who would lie down for Bart Simpson if pushed. You have been known to hide in stationery cupboards at the far-off clack of her slingbacks.

But you fantasize. *Oh yes.* She is tall but not too tall, willowy, blonde, full-lipped and has fingernails just long enough to titillate your naked back without leaving tell-tale marks. One day she will walk through the door and sit at the desk next to yours.

In the meantime you must make do with what the Good Lord has given you and they are a Vicious Bunch.

At your mum and dad's silver wedding the best man told how your dad pinched your mum's bottom in the typing pool and three months later they were engaged. If you pinched a bum in here you wouldn't be out of intensive care in three months, never mind engaged.

Not only must you not touch, you mustn't comment on appearance. 'That's a nice sweater' will get you a glare. A term of endearment or offer to help with a heavy object is taboo. You will be termed 'patronizing' or 'disgusting' and either ostracized or reported, depending on who you offended, and even the sensible ones are scared of letting down their side.

There are times when you can envisage the human race dying out altogether because no one will make the first move anymore.

'Work is something you do
when you can't stay in bed.'

And they don't play fair, because they look stunning, some of them. Well, who are they dressing for? And why the St Tropez tan and the highlights? Why douse yourself with Obsession unless it's to pull – and if that's the reason, why gaff the poor fish you land and throw him back?

Then they give you looks: you know, *meaningful*, gazing over the top of their modem. You know they're looking at you and they know you know, but what comes next?

I mean, you could send an email, just a simple 'Like to go out for a drink?' and find it spinning across the worldwide web. They gather round the coffee machine and giggle and you feel the hair prickle on the back of your neck because it could be you they're laughing at.

There've been relationships formed in your building because they got it right and picked a sane one, but it takes a Brave Man to chance his arm.

Besides which, there is the promotion thing. All you want is a level playing field. In fact, you are quite prepared to admit they got the short straw in the past. But that was then and this is now and now any bloke going up for a board with a woman of equal standing knows – KNOWS– *she* will get it because if she doesn't she'll scream discrimination and there'd be trouble. And then when they get it they do the smiley bit and hint that they'll be terribly gentle with you.

Sickening.

Now, there is a tendency to think that women talk freely about their sex lives while men discuss exactly how they would win football matches if only they could get on the pitch. I'm not privy to what goes on in the ladies' loo, but anyone who thinks men don't compare notes is seriously ill-informed.

So you sit smiling into your pint while they discuss the talent but you never pass an opinion. When pressed you give what you hope is a Gallic shrug. (You've never been quite sure what a Gallic shrug is but assume it's a combination of sophistication and vague disinterest.)

They get really worked up over the OFFICE PARTY, and judging by the tales there must be a certain letting down of hair there (one couple reputedly didn't surface for three days).

You had pictured yourself sauntering among the potted palms, working in ever-decreasing circles until you wound up at the side of the most attractive female present, but everyone has coagulated into groups: female staff in one corner, males in another; executives, male and female, in a third group with Personnel darting madly between saying 'Mix! Mix!'

No one moves.

The evening is as flat as the Champagne, which someone says is really supermarket cava with the labels changed.

You keep looking at your watch, convinced it's stopped or the battery's running down. Still, no one else is enjoying it either, except that you see Gordon – good old Gordon who still lives with his mother –

helping Emma, the MD's PA into her coat. For a moment you feel a pang of jealousy, then tell yourself that Gordon couldn't get it up in a harem and you just bet he keeps his socks on.

In the morning their faces tell a different story. Gordon looks ten years younger. Emma looks like the blue-tit who got the top of the bottle.

You might have bloody known! What did your mother tell you about dark horses?

You hang your jacket on the back of your chair, switch on your modem and ponder why everyone in the world is having it off but you.

That's when you hear screams from the Ladies. Some woman is crying and saying 'I can't face anyone'. Round about you everyone is bent over their work. This is odd because a scene usually gets rapt attention, but this is the morning after the office party, the biggest chickens-come-home-roosting session in the life of any workplace.

You start to work out the permutations of Who Slept with Who, who is flushed, who is wearing polo necks in spite of the heat ... you know the signs. It can happen to anyone.

Your day will come.

SHE SAYS... There's a statistic that says a high percentage of relationships originate in the workplace. That may be true, but it's not what you'd want, is it? Work is where you go to be thrusting and cutting-edge, thereby achieving rapid promotion and oodles of cash. You dreamed about it at university. It's called 'Getting On' and you were encouraged to see it as your goal.

None of this is compatible with winning the man of your dreams, who doubtless wants to see you as soft, feminine and weak as a drink of water. He doesn't want you to be the youngest executive in the building. He wants you to look like Scarlet Johanson.

'Genius is 1% inspiration and 99%
some other bugger's effort.'

Stories abound of women who slept their way to the boardroom but you don't believe them, largely because women at the top never have messed-up lipstick, much less a post-coital flush. No, if women make it as far as the glass ceiling you can be sure they *earned* it. One of these days a woman will bust right through it (OK, so you know about Marjorie Scardino but as a general rule...) and then it will be a fairer world.

Apart from which, men at work are almost always NERDS. They're either unkempt, odorous, beer-bellied and ambling towards retirement or they're spotty youths with desperately yearning faces and shoulders like wire coat-hangers under their jackets. Where the talent in the middle has gone to is anyone's guess. Perhaps some sexually voracious female executive rounds them all up and stows them somewhere to service her needs.

Not that it bothers you. You are there to work. You have a definite policy of non-fraternization.

You've heard the stories about office parties: the female who emerged from the Marketing Director's office with her dress on inside-out has been pointed out to you. You know whose bum was photocopied and flashed nationwide and who managed simultaneous flings with Publicity, Overseas Sales and Procurement.

You have difficulty facing everyone after you've been at an Ann Summers party so sexual shenanigans are a no-no, even in the event of anyone fanciable being around.

Although it worries you, you rather despise the men you work with. Before you came here, you heard tales of intimidation, women being brow-beaten, disadvantaged, exploited right and left. You were ready to deal with that, almost thirsting for the fight.

The reality is somewhat different. The women who are your line managers don't seem particularly on your side. The men aren't oppressors; if anything they have the hang-dog look of victims. You have a feeling you could buy most of them at one end of the street and sell them at the other at a profit and this isn't how it should be. Very few of the them are attractive and most of the time the women are either mocking them or roping them into relationships for the sake of it.

'All work is a circus act, except that at work the knife-thrower aims for your back.'

One day, you tell yourself, HE will arrive and he will be a SUD: Single, Upwardly mobile and Drop-dead gorgeous. Until that day comes you refuse to join in the gossip or the pursuit of any even remotely eligible man.

Roughly speaking, the female half of the workforce divides into two: The Desperate and The Politically Correct. The first lot spend their day emailing anything in trousers to say they've got tickets for Jamie Cullum and would he like to go; the second lot positively angle for a chance to slap a man down.

You don't approve of either tactic. You would rather scorch your knees with a blowtorch than lure a man with theatre tickets, and claiming you're a victim because some man admired your blouse is pathetic.

You despise women who scream rape because someone called them 'girl' or 'love' and the sight of some wretched man being flayed for an offence he doesn't realize he's committed is not pleasant. Besides which, it makes for awkwardness when you have to cooperate with a man on a project. You sense their unease but don't know how to calm their fears. You can't imagine yourself saying 'Call me what you like, I won't mind. Admire my jacket if you will, it's OK'.

You are appalled by trivia like this.

Is this what the Pankhursts died for? Well, they didn't actually *die* in pursuit of the vote but that won't stop them revolving in their graves at these goings-on.

And there's a part of you that is quite relieved that there's no talent around. It could be a bit of a strain fancying someone eight hours a day. Anyway, you want to get on – although with every passing day this seems less likely.

It's fairly obvious that women are advantaged at the lower levels because the bosses want to look PC.

But at the top, every single executive bar one is a man. In theory you could be sitting there eventually but you won't hold your breath. Still, if all else fails one day your SUD may come – but with your luck he'll probably be as gay as gay can be.

Deal with it

Sadly, the rules of the sports field, fair play and teamwork seldom apply in the workplace although they should. Accept this. Accept also that man vs woman should have no place in modern working practice. Perhaps she WAS promoted because she's female. Perhaps he WAS preferred because he's a man. If these are the only grounds for their advancement, they won't last. If they prosper, accept that they deserved it. Never use your sex as a bargaining tool. Concentrate on being the best and your day will come.

Holidays
Get away from it all. Alternatively, take it all with you

HE SAYS… Holidays sneak up on you when you're least prepared. For eleven months you promise yourself this will be the year of the BIG trip and then suddenly there's a week to go and you've arranged zilch.

You throw yourself on the mercy of a pneumatic blonde in a travel agency and find yourself at an airport clutching your passport and a folder that promises a two-star break in Ulan Bator. You sit in the departure lounge wondering why experience never, ever triumphs over optimism.

You *hate* holidays, so what are you doing here?. You've always hated them, ever since the family's annual break in North Wales. Sand in the sandwiches and sheets that smelled of mould. You used to look out of the window of your dad's Ford Capri as it toiled through traffic jams and promise yourself that one of the perks of growing up would be never to go on holiday again.

And here you are, waiting in a departure lounge in a terminal – well-named because another delay and you could lose the will to live. Even if you survive, sandy sandwiches cannot be far away. For this you've given up your life savings and left your car in an attended car-park so expensive it would have been cheaper to give the car away.

Why do you do it? Whatever excuse you give, at the bottom of it is the woman thing.

All men believe they'll go on holiday and meet a blonde with a PhD and a private income. Oh, they know all the pitfalls. How you can opt for a horny weekend and by the end of it she's entitled to half your pension. Or you swop phone numbers and find out her ex is a psychopath who can't tolerate anyone sleeping in his footsteps.

'A holiday is alright in prospect.
In reality it never fails to disappoint.'

And still you persist. Last year you vowed never to go abroad again. This was after finding the hotel was a building site and having a six-foot North African rob you of 75 Euros by sleight-of-hand in broad daylight.

And here you are, in a place full of foreigners and the only Brits around too drunk to focus. You decide never to go further than Whitstable again and fall asleep on a sun lounger, dreaming of Scottish lochs. You wake three hours later red as a lobster and so burnt you hear your skin cracking as you lever yourself to your feet.

Lying in a darkened room you realize it must have been a collective death-wish that sent young Britons off to colonize hot places. India, Africa, Australia – and all the time they could have stayed in Penge.

On the other hand *they* were *paid* to travel. You, poor fool, are shelling out to get third-degree burns.

And then you see the girl. She has long blonde hair – well, brown hair with streaks. She wears a sarong over a bikini and walks as though balancing a ewer on her head. If she doesn't perform 'The Girl from Ipanema' you'll eat your Piri Piri chicken baguette.

In fact, she comes from Huyton, works in a salad bar and has 'I love Becks' tattooed on her bum, although this is only hearsay at first because the sarong stays firmly in place.

You try not to pick at the peeling skin that surrounds the raw areas of your sunburn and make an effort to get her interested in modern jazz or ring-tones or Bichon Frises – anything at all that holds her attention. When she offers to put after-sun on your worst bits, only enormous self-control stops you from swooning with pleasure.

That night you decide it was worth coming after all. Three days later you're willing to put her on your car insurance. The following morning she's gone and so is your credit card. She's written 'sorry', in lipstick on the bathroom mirror and when you race downstairs you find she checked out three days before and your nights of passion were her bed-and-breakfast.

On the plane you decide to declare bankruptcy if she's gone to town on your card.

Back home you tell everyone what a marvellous time you had and cancel your card with your mobile while locked in the loo.

A man has his pride.

When the bill comes in she's only stung you for the fare home and 200 Euros of baby clothes. *Baby clothes?* You break out in a sweat until you realize she couldn't pin it on you, the latecomer.

The next afternoon you collect brochures for the Scottish lochs and vow never to leave Britain again.

SHE SAYS... Boxing Day you're hungover and still regretting the office party and your TV is full of white beaches, blue skies and hunky guys in speedos.

You close your eyes and dream.

The next day you buy *How to Learn Spanish in a*

Fortnight, and practice *olé's* in the bath. You also make weight-loss charts. If you go in June you have twenty-two weeks to lose three stone. Two pounds a week is reasonable, once you've eaten all the chocolate, Christmas cake and turkey littering the kitchen. On second thought you decide two stone are enough and you'll start January 15th.

You spend the rest of January visiting travel agents, but where to choose? Italy is full of buttock-gropers, France is full of Germans who get up at 3am especially to ruin your day, and any native French you meet will be virulently anti-British. Florida is thronged by people dressed as Mickey Mouse, Spain has more chippies than Blackpool... and for somewhere exotic like Honolulu you could buy a maisonette in Cheam.

If you're married or shacked up you ask the man in your life what he thinks. 'Holidays?' he says vaguely, never taking his eyes off the telly. 'Holidays,' you say firmly. 'You know, those things where you pack a case?' He shifts reluctantly and flicks channels. 'Right,' he says at last. 'Get on with it quickly, while there's nothing much on.' You tell him to sod off and lock yourself in the bathroom to dream of being the sort of woman who gets invited to private villas in St Tropez or Sardinia.

What a fool you are to contemplate holidaying with him.

There are men out there in Gucci loafers who know how to give a girl a good time. You're mentally sipping piña coladas with them on the Iberian peninsula when he knocks on the door and suggests you could kill two birds with one stone and spend a fortnight with his twin in Grange-over-Sands.

That's the last straw and you leave him, but the holiday problem goes with you.

You're a free woman so the sky's the limit, but everyone you know is already booked up so you'll have to go ALONE.

That's when you start remembering all those other holidays: the ones you've had therapy to forget.

You remember the utter awfulness of being together twenty-four hours a day for fourteen days and suddenly realizing you have absolutely nothing in common with the man in question. Sex in San Remo turns out to be terribly like sex back home: fleeting. Only this time you're coping with gyppy tummy and blisters from the sandals you should have broken in before you came but didn't.

Then there was the trekking holiday. It took four months for the saddle sores to heal. The time you camped the tent blew away and you had the only adventure holiday where the leader turned out to be a registered psychopath who led you all into quicksand.

So you throw yourself on the mercy of the guy in the travel agents. 'Where do you fancy?' he says cheerfully. He's looking at you through narrowed eyes and you have a terrible suspicion he's wondering if you're old enough for a Saga hol. You're digesting this unpleasant thought when he says it again. 'Tell me what you'd really like.'

'I bet he says that to all the tourists.'

What you'd really like is to stay in the flat for the whole two weeks with takeaways delivered hourly and every Brad Pitt DVD you can lay your hands on. But they wouldn't understand that at the office. You have to have BEEN somewhere or they look at you oddly when the snaps go round.

'You choose,' you say firmly and he opts for Grand Canaria because he gets extra commission on it this month. You write a cheque that has more front than substance and go home to pack.

The hotel is squeaky-new and looks like it was built from bubblegum. You lie by the pool and wait for romance to strike – except that the pool is littered with Angelina Jolie lookalikes who can eat three crème caramels at dinner and still wear tight jeans. On the whole they're unfriendly and the one who is forthcoming invites you to feel her boob-job. 'Only three grand,' she says cheerfully, trying to fish out a macadamia nut which vanished down a cleavage deeper than the Cheddar Gorge.

There are other things that throw you. Some people dry their towels *on bushes*. Others are merely extensions of their mobile phones and frown if you scrape your sun-lounger along the tiles. 'Hello?' they say into the phone, when they've finished glaring. 'No,' as they flash you a dirty look, 'it was just some idiot causing trouble.'

The three-grand boob-job has a new man every day and pleads the need for an early night by starting to yawn at 8.30 on the dot. You suppress your feelings of jealousy by biting your knuckles and wishing them *Bon nuit*. For the next few hours their lovemaking can be heard out at sea and everyone sits sipping Piña Coladas and pretending its native wildebeest rutting in the bush.

Eventually you face your reflection in the mirror and admit that some women look better half-naked than others. Next year, when you've developed the even peachy glow other woman have, you'll strip with the best. For now, you'll go cultural.

Three days of museums and you've had enough. There's only so much Byzantine art a girl can take.

You head back to Britain with your tail between your still-white legs. Only your face caught the sun – and you have the freckles to prove it.

Deal with it

We dream about them, plan them, pay through the nose for them but don't always enjoy them. Sometimes they fulfil their promise but seldom do they meet expectations. All holidays, however, broaden our horizons. Don't expect too much from them. You're more likely to meet your dream lover in the high street than the Arab souk, and an airline ticket is not a magic wand. See them as an opportunity to recharge your batteries and an opportunity to plan exciting things for the other fifty weeks of the year. And remember, there's always the bonus of coming home at the end.

Commitment

Those who want to commit often should be

HE SAYS… Commitment is a difficult word in more ways than one. Spelling it for a start. Is it two Ms or two Ts or one of each? And there's a finality about the word which can be chilling.

Oh, you may love the woman but you love a new car. You're even passionate about it, but the next year there's a *new* model. It's a sobering thought, isn't it? A motor you can trade in. A wife's FOR LIFE.

And you've noticed another thing. Once a man *has* a woman, once she's his officially, he seems to go off the boil. She becomes 'The Missus' or 'The Wife'. Once he couldn't get away quickly enough to meet her; now he takes to going to the pub after work and switching off his mobile when she rings. I've seen this in other guys more than once and it scares the hell out of me.

Men and women are different. Back in the 1970s when there was all that bra-burning, they tried to tell us there was no difference.

Well, that's *rubbish*.

We aspire differently. Women *want* commitment, even crave it. We *accept* it. Eventually.

Being financially responsible for someone else and resultant sprogs is more than enough to limit the libido. OK, they earn their own money now, but when it comes down to it you're the one behind the eightball if it all goes pear-shaped.

We even have different names for it. Women say they're 'in a relationship'. Notice that 'in'. They're in, you're in with them and the door's locked. Men say they're 'seeing' someone. *Seeing*. Now you see it, now you don't. No doors. No keys.

Women want to UNDERSTAND their man. A man doesn't *need* to understand a woman if he loves her. Men can be with a woman for forty years and be no wiser.

Men don't want to change their woman. Women are *dedicated* to changing their men. It doesn't make sense. It's like buying a Paul Smith suit and then cutting it up for vest and shorts. Expect interference, house rules: no more keeping ale in the bath or cutting your toenails in front of the telly. No more nights out with the lads which turn into days. No more sitting up all night to see the World Heavyweight Contest.

Go into any pub and you can pick out the committed men. Clock-watching, answering their phones every five minutes, downing their beer in a gulp because there's a casserole in the oven. Some of them have bunches of flowers with them. Before you can have a swift half with your mates you have to buy a sacrifice to the goddess of the home.

How's *that* for oppression?

And a woman doesn't have much tolerance for male pursuits. Unless she's your mother. Then she lets you keep your Scalextric in the front room and your maggots in the fridge.

'God created Adam and gave him Eden. Then he created Eve in case Adam was enjoying himself.'

Would a wife do that?

And once you commit, it's community money. Never again can you splurge on something daft; you have to convince the jury that it's sensible. Women have thrift boxes with compartments for all the different bills; they fill in their chequebook stubs and can tell you what margarine costs.

And then there's TIME OF THE MONTH. Pre-commitment you just avoid them when they go full-moon. Married, you have to live with PMT. You're stuck with it. (You're stuck all the time, come to that.) No prospect of getting trapped in a lift with Sarah Michelle Geller. You'll be round at your brother-in-law's helping paper the kitchen.

Humdrum, that's what commitment is. The end of adventure. The death of opportunity. Sod's law, the day after the wedding, the *very day*, you'll find the woman of your dreams at the next desk, across the aisle in a plane. And it will be too late.

We need women. That's indisputable. A hand on your brow when the going's rough, a meal on the table: they have their uses. But is a *licence* necessary? What happened to trust?

Nowadays there's another angle. She might be doing well. As well as you. Do you have the right to, say, give up the day job, bear the children? If she earns five figures and you screw it up for her, what a responsibility!

You could move in together, come and go, even have an 'understanding', but you both do your own thing. Except that women have this mad urge to pin things down. First the engagement ring, then the piece of paper. And they always win.

One day you hear a disembodied voice saying 'It's about time you met my folks' – and you realize it's *you*.

You shiver for a moment and then you remember all the men who went before and all the generations still to come. Who are you to buck the trend?

SHE SAYS... There's something sinister about the word 'commitment', like a door clanging shut. At first you dodge talking, even *thinking* about it, especially if you're still excited about having your own place after years of living at home or sharing.

Who wants to give up hard-won freedom?

Guys probably feel the same way. 'I'll call you' is a get-out half the time – and who cares because, like buses, there'll be another along any minute.

You look round your home and you feel like beating your chest and shouting 'Mine! All Mine!' Shutting the door of your own place against the world is better than sex – at least at first. When a woman realizes she's been seeing one guy regularly it shakes her. So much so that she might even panic and write him a Dear John, but she adds a smiley at the end just in case she changes her mind.

When he takes it on the chin and doesn't protest, she's first relieved and then peeved. Did he ever *really* care? Not that she cares, either. One day she'll want a man and kids but not yet. Her mother keeps talking about stability but she already has it: a salary cheque.

You know the feeling! You're good at your job and you pay your tab. You're a MODERN WOMAN. On a 25th birthday, however, a mother is liable to ring tearfully to say she hopes to live to see her grandchildren. As she's only 45, you can bear this reproach with equanimity. 'One day, Mother, one day'.

For now there's other fish to fry.

'Promises are like flowers and ice cream.
They have a limited shelf life.'

Friends mutter darkly about playing around and your mother may send you a framed, embroidered version of the old rhyme 'Too many rings around Rosie, Rosie gets no rings at all'. When this elicits no response she might start ringing weekly with tales of cousins' betrothals and women who discovered too late that they were infertile. She tells anyone who will listen that all her daughter cares about is her career.

Telling her that today women can have everything, just not all at the same time, doesn't work. Her eyes glaze over at the second sentence; she isn't listening.

This is when you look around the men in your life. Could you spend the rest of time with any one of them? Not unless ordered by the court!

Playing the field is fun, but the ticking of biological clocks is all around you. Mates you once relied on are popping out babies or hunting for William Morris tiles in junk shops because they're marrying an aesthete. A little voice in your head wonders if maybe time IS running out.

The same voice reminds you of the realities of cohabitation. Disgusting wet towels on the floor or, worse, on the bed. Underpants everywhere but the washbasket. Lager in the fridge, football wall to wall on television, and sex in the morning when you should be early at the office. No privacy to shave your legs or pumice your heels so they don't snag your tights. A disapproving male to catch you pigging out on munchies or eating taramasalata from the tub.

And quite apart from sex, mornings would be a *drag*. Men's faces improve with sleep. They look like little boys when they wake, even with stubble. Women's faces disintegrate, and even if you cleansed the night before, little rings of yesterday's mascara make you look like a lemur.

At times like that you want to be ALONE.

You had eighteen years of your mother breathing down your neck and two brothers clumping around like a first eleven. The prospect of voluntarily inviting a man to hog the bathroom does *not* appeal.

You know what you like. You know what you want. What you *don't* want is to share a bed for longer than an hour and a half. As for sharing your worldly goods, what you have you hold. And that goes for the duvet, too. (Men *always* hog the duvet. You read about it in magazines.)

So if men are funny and sensitive and intelligent and nice you steer clear. Shits are safer.

Occasionally in the wee small hours you get a fit of the jitters. You're 29 now. Your mother underlined it on your birthday card. You multiply the months between 29 and 35: 72. Times weeks + 288. Times hours. You give up when you come to seconds but 6,912 hours is a comforting total. There's plenty of time.

When the last of your best mates walks the plank you'll give it serious consideration. Till then, there can still be girlie nights out and the joy of the chase.

You get a pang when you see two people lost in one another or shopping together for what will be a meal *à deux*. So you remind yourself of flecks of shaving foam on the bathroom mirror, nail clippings on the bedside rug, dirty walking boots on your pale green carpet. You sniff the sweet, tangy air of freedom.

One day, Oh Lord – but not just yet.

Deal with it

Freedom is the thing we all prize. Commitment should never mean surrendering freedom. It does mean that some decisions will, in future, be taken jointly. It should not mean you have to ask permission to breathe. It does mean you have someone else to consider where before there was only yourself. It also means there is someone to back you, you no longer stand alone and that 'someone' has your welfare at heart. Consider very carefully before you make your decision but see commitment, carefully planned, as a door to opportunity, not one that will clang shut upon your liberty.

Moving In
Love and surrender (your possessions, your sanity, your remote...)

HE SAYS... You had no intention of sticking your head in the domestic trap. She's sweet, but women can change when you live with them.

Everyone knows that.

She keeps telling you two can live more cheaply than one, but what does money matter when liberty's at stake? In the end it's the boiler that clinches it!

You've listened to her burbling on for weeks about moving in together and a little voice in your head has gone 'Red Alert! Red Alert!' Let them do the domestic bit and you're done for: that's Lesson One in *The Bachelor's Bible*. Then your flatmate moves out and his cousin moves in and he brings a different women home every night and none of them are the silent type.

You stick all that and then the boiler goes. The first cold shower is bracing. You feel Spartan! The second day, after you've had the plumber's estimate, the lure of hot water proves too much.

Hell, you like the girl – *love* her, even. Why not give it a try? No more hiking home at 3am; no more finding what you need at her place is at your place and vice versa. You've no sooner said 'Well, maybe' than she has a lease on a place in Earl's Court in front of you and you've trod the dotted line.

And if you think a marriage licence is scary, a shared lease has all the charm of a boa constrictor.

Packing up is scary but you tough it out. You have a few tinnies with the boys before you actually go, but they're good lads and spoon you round to the new place in a taxi. You can't remember much about arriving except her saying she has a good mind to phone her mum.

Her *mum?*

What you didn't bargain for was her mum being part of the equation. And you certainly didn't know about the rule book. Before you moved in she was lovely. Pliable. Malleable. Accommodating, even. Once you share a roof you realize she wouldn't need training to govern Parkhurst.

You thought you knew women. *Knew* them? You haven't even smelled them. They're a law unto themselves – judge, jury and hangman. They have to have the last word in an argument. Anything you say after that is the beginning of another argument.

And she is never wrong. You haven't moved in with Miss Right; you've moved in with Miss ALWAYS

Right. If by any chance she's wrong, it's because of deliberate misunderstanding on your part.

And just when you think you're getting the hang of her rules, she changes them. Women can turn on a sixpence. You, on the other hand, are not allowed a rethink. When you walked through the door you left your rights on the step. Your name on the mortgage means diddly squat.

As for holding a decent conversation, a woman who thinks a striker is a trade unionist has no appreciation of the finer things of life. Then there's physical abuse. I mean, an elbow in the ribs when you're in a sound sleep has a touch of Guantanamo about it. *Everybody* snores, so why single YOU out? You don't give her the elbow every time she snores. And sometimes she can sound like a steam engine going up Snowdon.

'Genesis said it was not good for man to be alone.
Never trust the Bible.'

Still, the sex is good. The meals are even better. It's just the little things that grate. When last you lived with a woman you only needed to say 'I'd love a coffee' and it was there: hot and fragrant. Now you say 'I'd love a coffee' and she says 'So would I. Two sweeteners.'

Why can't all women be like mums? Your mother waited on you hand and foot and did it for love – the least she could do now is play along.

When did cooperation become a naughty word? You do your bit. Put stuff in the laundry basket, throw the duvet back to air, leave her some hanging space in the wardrobe, so why the need for 'His Jobs' and 'Her Jobs' on the board in the kitchen?

What more does she *want*? She has you in her bed – that should count for something. And why does her mother have to have her two pennies' worth?

Take this, for instance. You're watching a grudge match, Everton V Liverpool. Does she snuggle up in Time-out or a commercial (which would be OK)? NO. She waits until the centre-forward's taking a penalty and *then* she wants a snog.

Right at that moment!

When you fend her off (as gently as possible) she takes the hump and rings her mother. SHE comes round and does the 'You're not fit to kiss my daughter's boots' bit And when you choose not to retaliate, she accuses you of dishing out the silent treatment and changes the telly to The Discovery Channel.

She also moves your goldfish to the utility room. I mean, a sentient being that was used to company exiled to four bare walls and an instamatic. And SHE'S not even your partner; she's a guest in your home.

Seriously unwelcome.

Both of them bring up the toilet seat. If there's ever a World War III, the toilet seat will have started it. If they want you to put it down when you're finished, surely they should put it up when they're done. And the fuss over missing the bowl! Does it take two of them to deal with what is, after all, only modified H_2O?

Women CHANGE when you move in with them. She used to turn up, pretty as a picture, no fuss. Now it's 'Do I look alright in this?' and God help you if you tell the truth.

Still, all in all, moving in has its moments. She's cute in the morning, all sleepy and not a rule in sight. It's His Jobs and Her Jobs then, all right, and even she has to admit you're good. Besides, her boiler works a treat.

You have to be practical about these things.

SHE SAYS...The theory is that when cohabitation happens men feel regret for lost freedom. Women feel relief: home at last. That's the theory but is it true?

You've just got your place the way you want it, white walls, no clutter, soft lighting, the odd lily in a glass tube – and now *he* wants to move in! You always thought it would be special when someone moved in and he is special, in a way. But is he the MOST special?

How do you decide?

After all, choosing a mate is too important to be left to eeny meeny miney mo. But he is – well, *hunky*. Will he fit in? Once in will you ever get him out? Does he hog the duvet, which everyone says men do? Will he talk while you're watching something luscious on TV?

'Co-existence demands ignoring certain facts.'

You realize you know nothing about him at all. For forty-eight hours you panic. This is probably the biggest single decision of your life. You don't sleep, eat or answer his phone calls until he sounds like a little, beaten boy.

You give way and discuss.

Expenses, for a start? And space: you need your own some of the time. He meets you more than half way. In fact he meets you coming back. The prospect of not having to leave a warm bed at 2am is so intoxicating he'd offer blood if you asked for it.

You're touched by the degree of cooperation but you still have doubts. I mean, he's been in and out of the flat for ages but *living together*? That's DIFFERENT. No chance of snuggling down and waving goodbye at home-time. Now you'll have to leap out of bed when the alarm goes.

Naked.

Bra-less. The body has limits but the bra has none. (God bless lycra.)

> *'To co-exist it is sometimes necessary*
> *to shut one's eyes.'*

And then there's availability. At the moment he's gagging for you. Once you're on tap round the clock – official, more or less – will he stray?

You've just about talked yourself into it when he drops the bombshell. He's bringing his *dog*! A German Shepherd called Heidi. Dog? He hasn't got a dog. Oh yes he has. It's been at his mother's because his flat wasn't big enough and his flatmate has allergies but he's with you now and you have space and antihistamine to spare.

What do you do? Make like Cruella De Vil and bar the dog at the door or go out and buy Doggie-bytes?

It's a tough struggle but the Doggie-bytes win. He moves in and you sit on the loo the first night, after sex and a goodnight kiss, and wonder where freedom went. The fact that you have to put the seat down before you can sit on it does nothing at all for your mood, which is further depressed by the sound of whining and drooling coming from the bedroom. And that's only the dog. Can you spend the rest of your life in earplugs?

A week later, after his thirty-seven boxes and crates have been delivered, you discover his idea of helping with the chores is replacing the lid on the laundry basket. He eats flaky pastry in bed, flicks to Sky Sport during commercials so that you miss the vital few seconds of every Part Two and seems to have abandoned any form of romance other than the act itself. Where once he bought you flowers he now brings thick-cut marmalade 'because he always got it at Mum's'. When you ask if he prefers one outfit over another, he says 'Whatever', as though going out in a bin-bag would do.

Bitterly, you accept that this is married life and the absence of the licence doesn't make things any better.

There's also the time factor. When you lived apart he wanted to be with you every waking minute. Now, or so it seems, he's always 'just off out'. OK, so it's a pint with the boys or a game of squash but why the change?

You sit in your dream apartment, which now resembles a storage depot, and realize you've allowed a stranger to take over your life. Your best friend says 'Don't worry, it's not forever' and for reasons you can't quite fathom you burst into tears. Your mum rings daily to ask how it's going in tones that suggest she's already alerted the Apocalypse police. *His* mum, on the other hand, rings hourly to say she just forgot, but he likes his clothes well-aired and never give him prunes. You resist the impulse to infiltrate prunes into every meal but only because hospital beds are scarce and you might have to nurse him at home.

Instead you ponder the myth about moving in. They say men resist it, women crave it. The reverse is true in your case, and you give serious thought to the possibility that you're transgender.

You also loathe washing his smalls. On him they used to look white, taut and come-hitherish. Rescued from the tub they are greyish, sagging and *so* a turn-off. You also have to hide your 'comfy' knickers and just-on-the-turn white bras. Washday blues take on a whole new dimension.

You feel as though you're chained to the kitchen: no more deciding just to skip a meal. His mouth opens like a baby bird's at feeding time.

Then there's the phone. You can't moan to girlfriends about your leg wax or ask for zit tips. Superfluous hair and zits are for spinster establishments, you now live *à deux* – and it sucks.

Mornings have become ordeals. He sets two alarms on opposite sides of the room and leaps to each one before leaping back for sex. At first it's fun, but *every* morning? Another bone of contention is windows. He likes them open at night; you like them bolted against rapists. You like Radio 4, he plays Radio 1 so loud you'd think he was transmitting to the Hebrides.

You realize your nerve ends are getting ready to scream. But the real rub is job-sharing. You're being subtle about cleaning the loo. He doesn't do subtle. In the end you lock him in and won't let him out till it's done.

One day he gets flu, only he spells it 'pneumonia' if not 'bubonic plague'. He takes to the couch with a hang-dog look and the German Shepherd emits Baskerville howls each time he moves. You know this is because it hasn't had walkies. He thinks it's because the dog 'knows something' and death is imminent. When you ask if you should get a will form from the newsagents he accuses you of being flip. 'Flip' is not the word for what you feel; 'murderous' is nearer the mark.

When you get back that night the sink is full of mugs and bowls, he's drunk all the whisky and the dog has poohed by the back door. Worse still, he has moved the settee so he can see the telly better which plays havoc with your Feng Shui.

You take the dog out and come back to hear loud Australian laughter coming from your flat. (Australian laughter is quite distinctive, being louder than the European variety and more constant.) His Aussie mates have dropped round bringing grapes – only they come brewed in six-packs. He tells them you'll rustle up some sarnies if they haven't eaten and you wonder how prunes would be in a sandwich.

You're opening a tin of chopped pork and slicing bread when you overhear a remark, something about someone being a lucky sod and someone else being a beaut. Well, you're certainly not a lucky sod so you must be the beaut. You're oddly flattered but it doesn't stop you from ringing a date on the kitchen calendar.

You'll give him three more weeks. One to convalesce, one to adjust to the shock and one to move his crates and himself elsewhere.

You give them pickle with the chopped pork and even add a little salad garnish.

Deal with it

If possible, keep your own place for a week or two. This not only allows room to manoeuvre, it takes away that 'burned bridges' feeling and allows you to relax. If it's your place that will become the shared residence, accept that it is no longer 'your' place. You must accept change, not only in the surroundings but in house rules. Agree these in advance. If possible have two television sets, two radios. Establish a system for baths and showers; always being the one who finds the cold water is no fun. Above all, accept that everyone needs their own company sometimes. This isn't due to lack of love, it's the dear familiarity of two living as one.

Bad Habits
From Brad Pitt to Arm Pit

HE SAYS… Men are brought up to be self-contained. Even tough. We can't cast it off just like that, but women are obsessed with making us sensitive, talkative beings. 'Tell me this. Tell me that. What are you *really* thinking?'

Half the time you're not thinking anything. You're just enjoying sitting there with a blank mind because it makes a change from work. I call that harmless. Your average woman calls it 'a bad habit'. You've got to be switched on all the time or else you're neglecting them.

That's how unreasonable they are.

Your average woman could interrogate for Britain. They're merciless, and half the time you'd tell them if you could work out what it was they wanted to know.

They're also paranoid about your looking at another woman. I don't mean *lusting* after; I mean a simple look. They spell 'look' O-G-L-E.

Give them a ring and say you'll be late and you get the third degree. I mean, they *make* you lie. It's not that you don't *want* to tell them you're having a swift half with the lads, it's that they wouldn't believe you if you did tell them.

So you make something up about work and then you have to watch what you say all the time.

If they just trusted you, none of it would be necessary.

I'm also not that keen on make-up. Giving nature a helping hand is one thing; looking like the Dulux colour card is quite another. It comes off on your best threads and there's a cleaner's bill but that's *your* fault. By some magical osmosis you attracted the stuff to you. It's nothing to do with them – but if they never wore it, you wouldn't be smothered in it, would you?

Women labour under a permanent sense of grievance. You go to bed to *sleep*. You lie there, not harming a soul. The next minute there's an elbow in your ribs and you get the duvet torn off you till you're left with the cold bit that was on the floor. According to her, you're 'hogging' it. *Hogging?* How can you 'hog' when you're having REM sleep?

They say we snore. I've known blokes got taken to the doctor for snoring. Made to wear contraptions on their noses. *Divorced.* The unreasonableness of the female sex knows no bounds.

Take wardrobe space. The average woman has more clothes than M&S and two pairs of shoes for every item. You, poor sod that you are, have the cupboard under the stairs and split your head open every time you reach for some trousers, but you're accused of 'hogging' the space.

That word *hogging* again.

They're hinting you're a PIG.

It doesn't do to be sensitive around women. They have all this guff about our bad habits, but I wonder. I mean, how many muscles does it take to put a lavatory seat down – and do they *need* to scream at you to come and do it for them? Have you really invaded their space by peeing standing up?

A bathroom is a communal space, but you have no rights there. They ornament it with all kinds of fluffy covers and leave half-empty bottles and jars everywhere. If you take a dab of one after you've shaved or use it to soften some hard skin, they say it cost £75 a jar and you've 'contaminated' it. They could help themselves to anything of yours and you wouldn't mind.

That's what *really* hurts.

Women are also obsessed with neatness. Men fall into bed and sort things out in the morning. Women lay things out like sergeant-major's inspection. They have neat briefcases with initials on and inside everything's FILED.

That level of organization isn't natural.

Women can walk around holding the phone under their chin and yacking like mad while they beat batter in a bowl and keep their eyes on the telly at the same time. According to them, it's called 'multi-tasking'. To me, it's doing nothing properly.

It really pisses me off when they watch the TV and knit and hum tunes from *Mama Mia* and can still tell you who hid in the cupboard when the lights went out. You've never taken your eyes off the screen and you don't know, but they haven't looked and they do. There's no justice.

'Few things are more off-putting
than a good example.'

I've had relationships spoiled by female obsessions. Every woman is concerned the house will catch on fire at 2 am and she'll be busted if there's a teacup on the draining board.

You watch her while the late news is on and she looks really pretty. She's just had a bath and she's flushed and her hair's a bit ruffled and you get the urge. 'How about an early night?' you say, standing up ready for action. 'I'll just tidy up,' she says, and three hours later she comes to bed and expects you to still be lying there rampant. Male physiology should be a compulsory subject in GCSEs. There'd be less divorce if they knew what we go through.

They also TALK. Intimate stuff. A woman will tell another woman everything. And I do mean EVERYTHING. She'll be twenty minutes in a cloakroom with your best friend's woman and by the time she gets back she can tell you the colour of the inside of his eyelid. So you get the feeling the other women are all looking at you and know more about your bits and pieces than you do yourself.

Men talk, but most of it's hype. You never get personal. You just 'Ho ho' a lot and roll your eyes.

Talking of rolling your eyes: have you ever been taken into the middle of La Perla and then *deserted*? There's knickers right and left of you and twenty women between you and the door. I call that CRUEL.

I blame political correctness for most of it. If you decide to paint the fence without consulting her, you're a chauvinist. If she decides to paint the living room while you're on a course that means she's a liberated woman.

At work it's even worse. If you get a promotion, it's

favouritism. If she gets one, it's equal opportunity.

Next time I'm coming back as a woman. I mean, who wouldn't settle for multiple orgasms? Women have the ultimate weapon: they refuse you sex and you're putty. No one's died from lack of it, but lack of it makes you *wish* you were dead. That's where they have you and always will.

SHE SAYS... Men claim they are misunderstood. Women make vocations out of trying to understand them, but the success ratio is in inverse proportion to the task.

The reason we can't understand them is that we have logical minds so we can't grasp men's pathological need to own the biggest and best. Car, phone, DVD: you name it, they want state-of-the-art.

Mention buzz-words like 'professional' or 'new and improved' and he comes ALIVE. It springs from an inability to dissociate from childhood toys. The Hornby train set goes when they get four wheels. After that they collect car phones and video games and corkscrews that take six batteries to open a bottle.

This mad urge to possess is why you should never send a man to buy milk in a supermarket. He's constitutionally incapable of going through a check-out with a pint carton. He will have picked up a pair of jeans, a climbing pyracantha, a brace of guinea fowl and the eight-piece towel bale on special offer. Oh, and four packets of vinegar crisps and every size of battery in stock.

Another of their dainty little habits is a compulsion to dismantle things. Clocks, motorbikes, food mixers… in most homes there is something coming or going on the dining table, twenty-seven fiddly little parts that have to be shifted every time there's a meal.

'Most men are petrified adolescents'

Irritating as these may be, they pale into insignificance compared with their more sordid practices. I pass swiftly over passing wind from every orifice, a disgusting habit they think we should take as a compliment: a sign that they're 'at ease' in our presence. They also pick their noses and scrutinize the pickings. When they think no one's looking they wipe it on their sock.

What *really* gets me is their urge to stick a finger into whatever you're cooking, suck it, go 'Ooh' and stick it back for more. They have also been known to use your nail clippers to trim nasal hair and take soiled undergarments out of the dirty linen basket, spray them with deodorant and wear them for another day.

Women spend a lot of time and thought on dressing appropriately. No matter how often you buy men really sharp gear they will slouch around looking as though they've come to rod the drains. They're so besotted with their own wonderfulness they don't see the need to make an effort – and they are *incapable* of admitting they're in the wrong. The last man to admit a mistake was Pontius Pilate, and he washed his hands of it.

And they're bone-idle. The reason they have small, taut bottoms is that they sit on them all the time and the flesh compacts. (Not many people know that.)

I wish I knew why men pretend to like beer and drink gallons of it, but privately tell you they can't stand the stuff. And why do they want THEIR women to be Madonnas, but sit for hours in lap-dance clubs watching other men's women writhe around poles? They're not allowed to touch so they drool, and the more daring (and affluent) tuck treasury notes in the girls' suspenders.

The one thing you must never, ever do is let them make you a meal – not even a cup of coffee. They make it with water from the hot tap and the coffee doesn't dissolve and floats on the top and gets between your teeth so that when you grin you look like a demented crone. They have a mania for barbecues and feed you raw meat in a charred coating that smells of smoke. For the next four hours you keep checking your watch to see what time the salmonella will strike.

When they ring you they're terse, but watch them on a train. Men can start using their mobiles in Euston and still be yacking at Carlisle, and most of the time conversation will have consisted of boasts. When it comes to *talking* however, they hear the word 'commitment' and go deaf.

They are also selfish with the duvet and feudal with the remote control. Try a tiny little flick over to see what's on another channel and they scream they missed the best bit of the game. With this in mind, they take the remote with them when they go to the loo.

Even if you've got a dominant one he becomes a whingeing five-year-old at the onset of pain or fever. He's also rubbish at remembering dates. He knows Valentine's Day is coming for 364 days, but still scribbles a heart on a used envelope and tells you the card shop was shut.

That's because men have no sense of occasion. Great sex will be followed by an invitation to name goal of the week. How's that for post-coital technique?

Another failing is a complete lack of understanding

of shoes. Shoes are the cherry on the icing of couture, but he can't get his head round why you can't find one comfy pair and wear them with everything like he does.

Then there's THE LOO SEAT. Why does he always leave it up when you're going to need it down? Perhaps because men cannot multi-task. He can pee or he can manage the seat but not both together.

This is probably not their fault. Scientists know that more areas light up in a woman's brain than in man's. Most of his brain is unoccupied territory.

And that's why you love him, because you know he couldn't manage without you. And being needed is the biggest turn-on of the lot.

Deal with it

In the first flush of love, the object of our affections has no bad habits. As time goes on, this can change. That delightful little quirk becomes an obsession in your eyes. It can make you feel murderous. Ask yourself if it really matters. If it doesn't, learn to ignore it. If it does matter, speak out. If you do, however, be prepared to hear that you are not immune from bad habits yourself.

War Zones
I told you not to go down there

HE SAYS…When it comes to the car engine you're in the realm of the paranormal as far as women are concerned, but put them in the passenger seat, especially the *back* seat, and they come into their own.

Probably the first words Eve said to Adam were 'You're too close to the snake in front' or 'Do you *always* go as fast as this?'

Scientific studies have shown that men exposed to the female tongue over a prolonged period suffer damage to the cilia, or tiny hairs, in the cochlea or inner ear. Which is why most hearing aids appear on elderly men. Even when they don't speak they have ways of scaring you to death. You're driving along, cruising at a nice, steady speed – they let out a howl. Turns out they've seen a cat two blocks away and think you'll mow it down.

Men see the phone as a useful tool. Women see it as the power of ALWAYS BEING IN TOUCH. Men will sometimes shirk phone calls: what woman hasn't been asked to tell a man's mother he's not in? So men don't understand why women need to ring the friend they've just spent the weekend with and talk for an hour and a half. Men also resent women's ability to hold the phone in their neck while painting their toenails.

But the friction area that's a ten is SHOPPING. Shopping is the female equivalent of the hunt. Watch women at the sales: eyes gleaming with blood lust, jowls drooling, ready to tear a bargain limb from limb. Many of them suffer from the 'must have colour syndrome'. You know, they buy something in one colour and then just 'have to have' it in every other colour, even mauve, which does them no favours.

And then they can't wear the other colours because everyone will think they got them in a fire-sale.

'Your average woman has the face of a goddess, the mind of a spy and the hide of a rhinoceros.'

Men cannot see the sense in having something more than once – unless, admittedly, it's books on cricket or football or whatever your chosen sport is.

Control of the shopping trolley has led to many a melée in the past! Take a simple thing like mayonnaise. Does she want it with tarragon or mustard seed, the one with Paul Newman's picture on it or the own-brand cheapo? The time she takes pondering in the salad aisle, you could have made the bloody thing from scratch.

It's the same thing with shampoo. 'Is your hair listless or dry or dehydrated or bleached or thinning –?'

Sod it! Leave it dirty!

And don't even *mention* coffee. You buy the brand you've used for years and she tells you its mingled with the blood of peasants forced to pick beans for a pittance. Still, supermarkets are preferable to boutiques where you can find yourself in the grip of a sales-assistant who would sell her own bowel movements.

Women see shopping as a social occasion, with little oases in coffee shops, nice, shiny bags full of goodies piled round their feet. And then, when they get everything home, somehow it's not the same. The gloss has gone off. They sniff that perfume that sent them in the shop and say it smells like Toilet Duck.

Nor is it possible to understand MAIL ORDER. They browse through a catalogue where everything is displayed on sandy beaches and the models have skyscraper legs and look utterly, utterly at peace lounging on bits of driftwood. A man doesn't understand the romance of a catalogue or how shops can mesmerize women.

Research shows shoppers have a low blink rate, which suggests a trance-like state. That explains how women can kid themselves that not buying a £300 coat actually *saves* you £300 so you can afford those two dresses that are a snip at £150 each.

Shopping addiction is listed as an 'impulse control' disorder and there are times when you wish the men in white coats would suddenly appear, seize your woman and save you from wallet-destruction. Shopping is also a delusional state. Watch a woman trying to cram a size seven foot into a size six shoe in a sale and you'll know what I mean. All over the world there are women with crushed toes as a result of shoe sales.

'You have to learn how to live with someone in order to be able to live with yourself.'

Early on in relationships women will pretend to like sport. They'll stand for hours on a cold touchline blowing kisses when you score. So why are they dedicated to stopping you having the footie on and a few of the lads round?

Women. Now I come to think about it, there aren't many peace zones in the modern relationship.

That's what makes them interesting.

SHE SAYS... No matter how much in love you are, there are areas where conflict is likely to arise. Most of these involve objects or pursuits sacred to men. The remote control, their preferred sport, the car – especially the car. Men can be divided into three categories: Bachelors, Husbands and DRIVERS.

There's something about a long, shiny bonnet that twangs a man's cerebral cortex. Men have five different Y chromosomes, each paired to its own X. This makes them susceptible to the smell of petrol. They also react well to the smell of leather, particularly when it comes in the shape of driving gloves. Some have even been known to buy goggles and a helmet. This is known as Von Richthofen syndrome, after the baron of that name. They're also suckers for accessories such as jump leads in tooled leather cases or things for getting Girl Guides out of boys' hooves.

When drivers hit the mid-life crisis they start to drool over Harley Davidsons with alloy wheels, but until then, of course, it's CARS – and the faster the better.

If you want to hurt a man, criticize his driving. You can call him vain, egotistical, half-baked, acquisitive, even an anal-obsessive compulsive and he'll forgive you. Accuse him of a four-point turn and the tears flow.

The difference between the sexes is that a woman simply wants to get somewhere.

A man wants to DRIVE – so if he's lost what's an extra twenty miles? Ask directions? Did Columbus ask directions as he neared America? No. He sailed majestically on and that's what your average male driver will do, even when he's going due west and his destination is due east.

'What a man can't manipulate, he mows down.'

He doesn't ask for help because he can't admit he needs it. So he'll study the map and look knowing even when it's upside down and he's on the wrong page. Or he pretends he can navigate from the position of the sun and when it turns out wrong he accuses the council of moving the solar system.

But the most sport is to be gained from watching

him with the newest toy: satellite navigation. This gives him a little map on the screen and a patient female voice saying, 'At the third junction turn left.' He still gets it wrong but the patient lady understands men's little foibles. Quick as a flash she realigns: 'At the second junction turn right.' This should get him back on the right course, but does he listen? No. He tells her to shut up and starts darting down side roads as though he knew where he was going. This reduces the robot voice to a gibbering wreck because she keeps trying to right his wrong turns.

When you point this out, you get a tirade.

'That's right: put *me* in the wrong again! YOU do it if you're so clever!'

You both know he'd rather donate an organ than let you behind the wheel, so all you can do is turn up the radio and settle down for a nap. It doesn't pay to ask why he bought an expensive gadget he doesn't intend to use. They brought it out; he had to have one. This is because men never grow out of their obsession with toys.

Once it was a Dinky, now it's a Merc. No difference.

Similarly, everything electrical they buy has to be complicated. The On/Off switch is neat and practical, but that doesn't do. Men have to have extra fiddly things:

anything with flashing lights, anything that beeps. If they made a juicer with an inbuilt flight simulator or a ringtone, that would be right up their street.

If men were honest they'd admit that the garage is their favourite room in the home. They like its greasy, testosterone-laden smell and the noise as they race the engine for hours while staring moodily into the engine and occasionally twiddling a nut.

When a man returns to the house after one of these contemplative sessions, he'll make straight for his phone or Ipod or the remote. He *has* to hold something that goes on and off. (Remember what Russell Crowe did when his phone wouldn't work? He got arrested…)

It's the same in traffic jams. He can't lie back and think of England. He'll race the L and R electric windows, check the rear-view wipers, drum on the dashboard, pull out the lighter to see if the element is red.

His power complex means he has to *own* the remote control. Women who live with a man should insist on two televisions. It's not that men are selfish. It's just that in a one-set household a woman must wait until she's widowed to discover there's more to life than The Sports Channel.

A woman has no sooner picked up the remote to change channels than he says 'give it here' in pitying tones and wrests it from her. Then he gets four wrong channels and tries to convince her the last one is the one she REALLY wants to watch.

'Distrust is the only defence.'

Men have been known to take the remote to the loo or hide it up their sleeve and pretend it's lost, which leads to women crouching in front of the set to operate it manually. This won't stop him scanning 52 channels in five minutes but it can interrupt the flow if her finger is faster than his.

You can also frustrate him by using his tools, especially his power drill. A six-foot man will be reduced to a snivelling four-year-old who wants his ball back if you do that. He may even offer to arm wrestle you to see who should have use of a particular tool. If anything is even vaguely technical he thinks it's his province and you – poor addle-brained female that you are – wouldn't understand it's complexity.

Another pistols-at-dawn area is shopping. To men, shopping is not a sport, it's a CHORE and nothing is going to convince them otherwise. That's where they differ from women. Men don't need more shoes, clothes, gadgets – correction: maybe the odd gadget or two; always room for more.

It's no accident that department stores are designed so that bed linen or handbags or jewellery – all the things that will draw the female half of a couple – are strategically situated next to the electronic or sporting equipment. Unless let loose in one of these areas, a man's shopping is over in ten minutes so he can get home ASAP for the footie. Women's need to try everything on, whether or not they want to buy it, simply mystifies men.

Watch a man shopping. He looks like someone with a price on his head. The average man has three pairs of shoes, two pairs of jeans, some sweatshirts, a suit and a jacket in his wardrobe. He doesn't feel compelled to buy the suit in three colourways or have matching shoes. So he'll never understand a woman's needs.

There's no point in asking a man to buy feminine products for you. The most confident will baulk at asking for sanitary wear. Tell him shampoo and he'll bring back conditioner ('Well, the bottle's the same shape…').

And they have crazy ideas about time! You go out at Christmas to buy for your large combined families and when you come out of the first shop he says hopefully, 'Is that it, then?'

But the real no-go area is wallpaper. Try explaining mood or ambience to a man in a wallpaper shop. It's like draining peas through a wrought-iron gate. Except they do seem to gravitate to Stringfellow decor: red velvet chairs, lots of gold, chandeliers. All you need is a pole for slithering down and you'd have his natural setting – but you point this out at your peril.

It's not uncommon nowadays to see couples do the supermarket shop together. He's OK in charge of the trolley but should never be set free on his own. Men go in for bread and beer and come out with a groaning trolley which they still try to bring through Five Items or Less.

They're suckers for three for the price of two or the special-offer bog roll that no woman would buy (it's so thin you need 27 sheets for a decent mopping up) but fear of being called a tightwad prevents them from comparing prices. Women take pride in being called thrifty; men are ashamed of it unless they're accountants, in which case they check *everything*. Numbers of stairs, organ pipes, birds on a picket fence –

an accountant can accompany you to the check-out and tell you the bill will be £87.40.

He's never wrong.

Men and shops simply don't go together. He'd far rather spend a day on the touchline cheering on his team. Whatever his sport, that's where he comes alive. On his way to a match he'll incline his body forward in his eagerness to get there – like women do that when they're nearing Harvey Nicks. This dog-like devotion to sport is what causes friction. A woman wants to be No. 1 in a man's life and not come second to Arsene Wenger.

The internet is another bone of contention in the average household. Men love all their little secret files and putting locks on things so the mouse can't access them. No woman can tolerate a locked room, not even in cyberspace.

And apart from the worldwide web, animals fill a big space in a man's life.

Diamonds are said to be a girl's best friend.

Dogs are Man's.

I ask you, which sex is smarter?

Dogs give you unconditional affection and don't sell their story if you let them sleep with you. They don't try to outsmart you and the worst thing you can catch from them is fleas. With men it's 'Love me. Love my ferret' and the wise woman never tries to come between them.

She knows when she's beaten.

Deal with it

There are certain areas where two competing wills are almost bound to clash. It can begin with something as simple as who controls the remote and end in the divorce court. So eliminate the dangers. Have two televisions if possible, and respect for the other's preferences if not. See shopping as a one-man or one-woman operation wherever possible. Love has died more than once keeping vigil outside a changing room. You may be the better driver but don't rub it in. If your partner sees the telephone as an extension of their arm, so what? There are worse crimes. Tolerance is the lubricant of good relationships.

Money
Liquid assets have a way of leaking

HE SAYS... When you decide to move in together you never think about money. Well, not *really* think, beyond paying the moving van and a modest housewarming to celebrate.

Money doesn't scare you. You've tightened your belt before. At uni you once went three days without a proper meal. If it hadn't been for the nourishment in beer you could have done your system an injury.

If you were moving in with a gold-digger or an air-head it might be different, but she is sensible about money. Right from the start she paid her share. Now, with two salaries and only one roof, you'll both be quids in.

Except that no one tells you removal firms rip you off and two into one won't fit and your rowing machine will be out in the street for two hours because there isn't an inch of space inside.

The upshot of it all is that you have to move somewhere with more space. You find the perfect place but she says the bath is too small. You're perfectly happy with a shower but women use the bath to PLAN.

That's why they're in there so long you have to knock on the door in case they've drowned.

While they're replacing the bath it seems silly not to have a bidet and new taps all round and a screen instead of a curtain for the shower. The resultant plumber's bill makes more than your eyes water. But not as much as the bill for the new sofa, without which, apparently, neither of you can exist. And if bidets and sofas can be afforded, why does your picking up a copy of *Autocar* lead to a sharp intake of breath on her part?

'Don't let anyone pick your pocket with her tongue.'

The answer is that you've shacked up with a closet chartered accountant and a high-maintenance chartered accountant at that. Your hard-earned cash now goes towards haircuts, facials, manicures and sessions where she goes in pale as a lily and comes out with a Bahamian glow. When you utter a mild query about costs, she wags a perfectly manicured finger at you.

At least you're being mugged by a stunner.

One of the most exciting things about women is

their inconsistency. I mean, men are relatively straightforward. Supping, shagging and sport (not necessarily in that order) that's the male psyche. Women are different and yes, *vive la différence*, but you have to concentrate to understand them. The woman who uses a calculator to work out the exact – *exact* – price of a pat of butter has a designer handbag stuffed with 10p-off coupons. She keeps them 'just in case'.

Bizarre if you ask me but, like I said, that's what keeps you fascinated. If we cracked the way their minds work we might go off them and that would be tragic.

You find you're worrying about money more than you did before, which is strange when two can live more cheaply than one, but when she kisses the back of your neck, the whole thing floats into perspective. Then she shows you a jar where she's saving twenty-pence pieces 'for the future'. In future there'll be money for everything, even a season ticket to Arsenal.

This inspires you to go through your change and hand over four of the little coins. 'There, now,' she says in satisfied tones and you realize that her teeth are just the tiniest bit Transylvanian and why have you never noticed that before? Still, they're charming, especially when she uses them to nibble your ear.

All you want is a nice, aspirational, middle-class life. Not too much debt. A mortgage, a card or two and the odd overdraft for holidays. And a decent car because the one you have now isn't really meant for two, not with the amount of luggage she travels with. You don't see eye to eye about the car because she says a nice saloon would be best and you want to keep just a hint of Man About Town. Besides, you couldn't fold your legs into a Ford Focus and you won't contemplate amputation, not even for her.

You have a bit of a spat over cars. She keeps harping on about the cost of petrol and gas-guzzling cars and how she's willing to surrender a lot for you but children eventually is not negotiable and have you any idea how much babies cost?

Up to now you've done an excellent job of not allowing yourself to think how much babies cost because the mere thought brings you out in hives.

That night in bed you lie and think. You love her: no doubt about that. But there's this *thing* – this house, home, dwelling growing up around you. His and hers, shared possessions.

What if it came to a break-up? You have a vivid mental picture of taking a chain saw to the bidet and the sofa ('You want half? I'll give you half!') You've heard of men being driven to do that, even sawing a whole house in half once.

And you suddenly realize how well your folks got on.

They never had much money but somehow they coped and you feel a wave of affection for them, stronger than you ever felt before.

'If you're not careful, two can live as cheaply as three and a half.'

And somehow that makes you feel differently towards her. More tender, especially when she empties out her twenty-pence pieces the next night and says they're for 'syncopation'. Translated, this means 'rapid movement from bar to bar' because you can't buy more than one round with twenty-pence pieces without them giving you funny looks.

You cave in then and decide to get rid of the gas-guzzling car. She's very loving afterwards because she's touched at your sacrifice and once more you give thanks for your luck.

You'll never have to worry about bills mounting behind the clock or late-payment charges on your card. You've picked that rare combination, a woman who's good in bed and has a head on her shoulders.

Like she says, a Porsche is not a family car.

Perhaps you could test-drive a Mondeo. You'll ask about it tomorrow.

'Between the dream and the reality
sits the bank manager.'

SHE SAYS… You fall in love and suddenly it seems madness to live apart. After all, two can live as cheaply as one. One rent, one central heating, one council tax… and everyone knows you never eat when you're in love. You'll save a fortune.

You discuss it – not that there's anything to discuss because you're in complete agreement. 'We love therefore we share' is the mantra. So there's no need to go on and on about money, but it's only logical to plan income. I mean, a child costs you £200,000 by the time it reaches twenty-one. That's a government figure – well, official anyway.

And there are lots of areas where you can economize. Basically, every purchase should have a

POINT. Buying *House Beautiful* has a point to it – you get ideas from it. All *Loaded* gives you is ideas you'd be better off without.

And two morning papers is positively foolish. It's the same news in both and he never reads the political bits.

Like all men, he's childish about cars. It's a penis thing: who's got the longest bonnet and the most horsepower. There's no need for him to feel sensitive; he's very good in bed and you tell him that often enough.

And you do your best to save. You have to spend money on grooming because it's essential to your job. When you're at home with children you'll save piles because you'll do everything for yourself. Who wants a French manicure when you're washing nappies? And you *will* wash them because disposables are ruining the environment.

What's difficult is working out what's essential and what isn't. Men are stupidly generous sometimes. Ridiculous tipping! And he can't go into a shop for a single item; has to come out with his arms full.

But deep down you're very alike. You don't want a life of debt-juggling and conspicuous consumption and neither does he. And you both want children and there's no escaping the cost there. At the moment it's building the home, getting things nice. You could have managed with the old stuff – his and yours – but once you moved they just didn't look right and you won't be able to splash out once there's a family.

There's the world of difference between meanness and running a tight ship. Writing everything down makes sense – you can see where the money's going. That's how you found out about him joining the Lib Dems. Which is a total waste of hard-earned cash because they'll never run the country. Still, it's *his* choice and everyone's entitled to a little mad money.

'Whatever comes between us, it won't be money.'

You said that at the beginning and you mean it now.

You once told him about that friend of your mother's who made her husband pay for sex. I don't know how much; it was old money when she started. Anyway, she banked it for years and years and then when he retired she left him. Took the money and ran. You told him that story just to show him what some women are like.

'Do you take plastic?' he said, which creased you both so you allowed him a freebie...

The trouble is that men don't get the concept of *waiting* for things – don't accept that money has to be prioritized. Season tickets are fine once everything else is attended to, but who wants to skulk indoors in a Chelsea shirt with the curtains drawn in case the bailiffs come?

Sometimes, when PMT strikes, you wonder if he'll love you forever and what would happen to all these possessions if you split up. Still, they're only *things*. He could have them because if he left you you'd be so distraught you wouldn't care.

It would be different if it was a dog, but possessions are just possessions.

It's a mystery where money goes. You thought you'd be swimming in it when you got the move over but there's never anything left over at the end of the month.

It's true what they say about yours being the IPOD generation. IPOD as in Insecure, Pressured, Over-taxed and Debt-ridden. Fortunately, everyone you know's in the same boat and that makes it easier to bear.

And it's worth it, really. You can't spend like you used to or go to New York to shop twice a year but you're building a future, aren't you? And you do manage to save a little bit – although it usually gets squandered on a night out when you're both fed up.

Still, what's money for if not to spend it together?

And you do love him to bits.

Well, you *will* – when he gets a sensible car, one with room for a carry-cot in the back.

Deal with it

Money is too important to be left to chance. Unfortunately, when we fall in love meaningful discussions about money seem almost obscene. That doesn't stop them being necessary. If you have an agreed strategy, arguments and resentment are less likely. It's unwise to assume all money will be communal money. Each partner has a right to something of their own to waste if they choose and if they've been used to financial independence they may still wish to retain an element of it. Decisions on money jointly saved should be jointly made. A relationship is not a business but it still needs boardroom discussion. However much love there is, you need to use your head. Saying 'I don't care about the money' is not enough. If you want things to run smoothly, learn to care.

Friends
A friend in need is a bleeding pain

HE SAYS… It's funny how sometimes you just click with a bloke. Almost instant. It has to be chemical because you don't yet know that he'll share your values, your sense of humour, your passion for cricket and take the same size in shoes. You just know he's a mate.

There's something about male friendship. Women cling on to each other and giggle and whisper and tell one another every bleeding thing.

Men aren't like that.

He comes back from a hot date and the most you'll say is 'OK?' He gets a beer from the fridge and rubs his nose before he replies. 'Yeah,' he'll say, reflectively rather than enthusiastically. On a scale of one to ten that's an eight, but you don't go all swoony on the sofa and do the 'and then what did she say?' bit.

He's had an alright night – and that's all you need to know.

Next month you'll be at Moss Bros getting kitted out because her mother wants the wedding in the *Leatherhead Gazette* but there's no need to chew it over now: not when Lineker's on the box.

Male friendships *last*. You can go right through school with someone then move to the opposite ends of the country, not see one another for four years and when you meet up he'll remember exactly what you drink and your first car reg and how many sugars you take in coffee.

'Ask no questions of a friend. When they're ready they'll tell you all you need to know.'

Real mates don't fight over women, either. They might fight for one in a Hollywood film but in real life you go down the pub and by the time you've sunk a couple of pints it's settled. You toss for who'll tell her and then book up for white-water rafting in Wales.

No woman's worth the loss of a mate.

Men are good at the class divide, too – well, *real* men are. You can go up in the world, make a fortune, get a gong even, and your mate's never paid higher rate tax, he drives a Ford and lives in a semi, but you still meet up regularly. You may run your own company; he only majored in woodwork – but you both play five-a-side and that's enough.

Women can't do that. They need TRAPPINGS and they have to be seen around other people with TRAPPINGS . The best they can do for a friend from the past is a furtive coffee in a Starbuck's. And when they get home they'll talk about 'Poor little Debbie: so sweet in her M&S.'

Does a man give a toss what a friend wears? Never! Cars are different, but you don't begrudge a mate a Merc: you're proud of his achievement. And he'll let you get behind the wheel. You don't see women sharing like that.

Look back at history. All the great friendships were men. Saul and Jonathan, Damon and Pythias, Butch and Sundance... can you see two women holding hands to jump off a cliff? Well, all right, so there was that *Thelma and Louise* flick, but that's more of an exception.

On the whole men don't betray other men. In business, maybe, because that's the name of the game. But your average man'd go to the stake for a buddy.

You see it in your local football crowd. There's a solidarity there that women can only envy. Men are faithful to one another. It's like in war: you stand shoulder to shoulder and you feel confident because that's a man at your back. OK, the enemy's masculine, too, but you know what I mean. When the chips are down you can't beat a man-to-man relationship.

We can be mates in spite of differences. You don't need to know his views on politics or even his middle name. He may tell you – well, when he's had a few drinks he'll force the info on you – but you don't NEED to know and that's the difference. I mean, if you want deep conversation, form a book club.

And men know how to let their hair down with their mates. Beer-can roulette's a kind of bonding ritual. So are embarrassing stories and shouting and playing cricket with a 4X can and having a bloody good time. Letting rip. It's like saying: 'I'm *alive*, man!'

But underneath, when there's just the two of you, you can sit and look at a glass for hours. Or have a smoke. Or talk about the weather. Or the beautiful game. Just quiet friendship.

No woman can give you that.

Men don't fall out like women do. That always amazes me about women: they're thick as thieves and then suddenly it's Ice Age.

'What happened?' you say, expecting incest or rape or at least a hit-and-run.

'She criticized my bag.'

That's *all*.

A simple little remark about a piece of suede and the balloon goes up. A man can tell you he's slept with your sister (your mother, come to that; it does happen). You're miffed. I mean, there *are* limits. But he says 'Sorry, mate' and sticks his hand out and you shake and he gets the next round in and it's never mentioned again.

'Some friendships are undeserving of the name.'

It's not in the female psyche to deal with REALLY BIG THINGS. They operate on a different level.

And they don't really understand friendship.

That's a *male* thing.

All they same, mates can make for complications when it comes to serious womanizing. They'll clear off and let you make a hit alright because they don't expect it to last. You'll have two weeks of bliss and then it'll be back to the pub and pints all round.

When you realize this one is different, it's a funny feeling. For a while you wonder if it's worth disrupting the status quo: Friday nights, the odd trip away, the match… you've seen your brother-in-law condemned to bag-carry in John Lewis when he could be at the ground. Sod that for a game of soldiers.

Besides, you don't fancy telling them. They gave you leave of absence, now you're contemplating going AWOL. You know how it'll be: they'll pretend to be pleased but they'll be wounded to the bottom of them because you've broken faith.

And SHE doesn't like it when they're around. You can see her squaring up, ready to claim territorial rights. I mean, they're used to dropping by – they're your MATES. And they only stay for a jar. SHE has friends – or she *did* have.

They seem to be keeping their distance, except when they sidle up and drop the poison. Witter, witter, witter and she gets that look in her eye, like a pregnant hamster. First time you're alone it's: 'Jan says' or 'Jan thinks'…

Jan should butt out, in your opinion.

That's the difference between men and women: all girl babies are born with a spoon in their hand and they never let go.

Male friendship: you can't beat it.

SHE SAYS…What would life be like without friends? Less complicated for a start. If you read women's magazines you'd think that women are all matey and confiding and giving one another face packs and painting one another's toenails and swapping sex tips. Well, yes we do all that, but usually it's with best mates, not the wider sisterhood.

Being female doesn't automatically mean you *gel*.

Take changing rooms, for instance. I don't feel free to walk about in the nuddy because we're all girls together, even if they're friends of mine. I'd sooner disrobe in front of men. Their eyes may go funny when you unpeel, but at least they're not calibrating your cellulite and nudging someone to say 'Get a load of *that*'. They're not friends really; they're acquaintances.

Even your best friend, the one you met in nursery and have clung to through thick and thin, can cause you problems. You go on holiday together each year, which necessitates you starve yourself from January 14 and still she manages to make you look like a well-used bean bag. Slim as a reed, brown as a berry, perfect toe and fingernails... you should have pushed her off the slide at nursery and broken her front teeth, which, like the rest of her, are unforgivably perfect.

Except that you couldn't live without her. Who else would come round with Kleenex at 4am because you've been dumped and cried your way through all the tissues and loo roll in the house?

'Good friends give you room to grow.'

The trouble with friendship is that no one has yet defined where friendship ends and total dependency begins. Beware the friend who rings up 'just to hear your voice'. Be warier still of the 'best' friend who befriends your boyfriend and proceeds to psycho-analyze you to him and him to you. Before you know it, she'll have persuaded you that he's a psychopath and him that what he really needs is a roll in the hay with her. When that's accomplished, she'll shudder with self-righteousness when you threaten to bash in each of her two faces and tell you she only did it to prove to you that he was incapable of being faithful.

Worse still than the Double-Crosser is the Control Freak. She will wind up directing your life, telling you where to in- and exhale, who you can talk to, where you can eat – she wants to control your coming in and going out, and nine times out of ten she'll get her way.

When you're a teenager you put up with all this because the thing that most terrifies you is being left friendless. As you get older you learn to pick out true friends and hang on to them.

The real trouble starts when you fall in love. Before that fatal moment, your friends were on call for you 24/7 and you them. Now, while you still care about friendship, every fibre of your being yearns to be with HIM.

The trouble is that while you're prepared to put your friends on the back burner temporarily *his* friends can't take a hint. At times you feel they'll pop up from under the duvet and say 'That was nice!'

Men don't major in sensitivity.

I mean, they might not be able to help arriving with tinnies and a copy of *Loaded* but once they see you on the couch you'd think they'd make a graceful retreat.

You'd think that!

In reality they blunder in, congregate in the kitchen, get louder and louder and generally ruin your well-planned evening. And HIM mouthing apologies and hissing 'I'll get rid of them in a minute' is no help at all.

Women wouldn't do that. They'd take in the situation

at a glance, make some charming excuse and waft away.

Well, some of them would. I have known women who could cling to a blade of grass in a force ten gale. But they have to be dealt with. And the good ones always understand.

Be honest: would *you* put a friend first if it came to a man? She rings and says she's just fallen through the ice and hypothermia beckons. You're on your way to a red-hot date. You'd like to think you would run straight there with a lifebelt and a thermos but cold realism says you'd tell her you were stuck in an elevator and could she call the RAC.

> *'Fairweather friends have a habit of dissolving if it rains.'*

And once you're settled you can still have girls' nights. They haven't gone for good. Which is why it's hard to understand why HE still needs the male-bonding thing on a constant basis. Still, enduring his friends is the price you pay for love and some of them are OK.

In small doses!

When a man comes along it can affect friendship in

other ways, too. You can't have a good old bitch down the phone with him earwigging a sofa's length away. And you can't have that one drink after work that turns into a session if you've got to run home to grill his chops.

You should never tell a friend that your man flosses his teeth to the sound of salsa music or wears a Chelsea shirt for heavy sex. No friend could keep a gem like that to herself. Except a best mate, of course. She tells you everything and *your* lips are sealed.

When the red-hot lover has dumped you and you're out of cigs and your best mate comes round with a bottle and 20 Silk Cut there's no feeling like it.

You can snivel to a friend, wiping your nose on the back of your hand while you tell her what a sod he was and she nods wisely and says she knew it all along and besides he has bandy legs – which you've never noticed but now she's pointed it out, it helps. You can't do that with your mother or a counsellor without them telling you there are better fish in the sea, which is the single most unhelpful phrase in the English language.

And true friends never point out that only yesterday you were boasting he was the World's Greatest Lover and faithful unto death.

True friends have discretion as a middle name.

Nor do they tell you to stop the self-pity. Self-pity is nature's balm. A real friend never says you should stop crying and go on a weight-loss diet. She instinctively knows that being red-eyed and fat is right for this particular moment. She makes you a milk shake with full cream, laces it with Tia Maria and hands you a loo roll, which is better than tissues in a real crisis. You don't have to pretend with mates, either. You can let your tummy sag, chew your nails, wear your saggy old ski pants and a thermal vest and it doesn't matter.

If they're true friends they'll level with you. When you look them in the eye and say, 'Tell me, is it true?' it's a good friend who says, 'Yes, it's true, but she's not a patch on you.' You can have a good cry then until she makes you laugh by telling you the other woman has an arse the size of the Albert Hall and shaves her moustache with a blow-torch. You both know it's lies but it's friendly lies. Comforting lies: the kind only a friend can tell.

You can find fault with almost every friend but you still need them.

Who else will squeeze your hand while you do a pregnancy test or lie for you when the need arises? Who else will rub your back when you have period pain or swap earrings with you on the way into a party because you'll look better in hers than she does?

Yes, a friend like that is to be prized above rubies.

Each adult entering a relationship has history. Friends are part of that history. Hopefully, they can be enjoyed. If not, they must be endured because they are an integral part of the person you love. Start to chip away at history, and you risk wounding not only your partner but the relationship itself. If the friends are yours, loyalty to them is laudable but once you embark on a relationship you have to give weight to your partner's needs, too. Cherish friendships, but if you want your relationship to last, make sure they don't intrude into areas that are meant to be intimate. Hopefully, friends and lovers can co-exist. It's up to you to see that they do.

Infidelity
Sex now, pay later

HE SAYS… The latest craze is 'Intelligent Adultery'. It's an American thing and put simply it means 'Don't get caught'. If nobody knows, nobody gets hurt – that's the theory.

The trouble is that 'intelligent' is not the word to apply to adultery. You're *bound* to get caught and when you do, the ordure hits the fan big time.

Adultery makes you crazy. City bankers climb into bed with the nanny and only plasterboard between them and the marital bed. What makes them do it?

Personally, I think adultery is a form of paranoia. Why else would a man risk home and children and his mother-in-law's tongue?

OK, it comes in degrees. At first you think you will just nibble at the edges. Where's the harm in a kiss? But flirting is adultery's nasty little sister. Stick at it long enough and you experience meltdown; after that you're on auto-pilot. Forget vows and marriage lines and alimony. What man on the brink of meaningful sex has ever said to himself 'I'll pay for this'?

But pay you will.

The hair-trigger of your libido will cost you dearly.

Leaving money aside, why does a man who has a charming woman at home bed a ball-breaking colleague who would do him down as soon as look at him if it came to the chance of promotion?

One theory is that all sex is rape. But who is raping who? When you succumb to that wide-eyed secretary who reminds you of your sister but has mesmerizing breasts, did she get you into bed or you she?

You tell yourself no one will suffer. Not her, not your partner, not your children. Because no one will know. The adulterer is an illusionist who puts David Copperfield to shame. Male or female, they are their own audience.

'Adulterers are like politicians: they think they can fool all of the people all of the time.'

You plot like Agatha Christie, explaining away absences with an ease that shocks and then thrills you.

You're GOOD at this.

All the same, you have moments when you break out in a sweat: like the time she gets to your overnight case before you do: 'Just taking these for the wash, darling.' What if there is something illicit there – female paraphernalia? You get up at 2am to rake through the wet stuff in the tumbler. Stubbing your toe on the way back to bed brings tears to your eyes

At times your loved one is so sweet you swear she has found out and is heaping coals of fire upon you. Her eyes are innocent, her mouth trusting. She feels loved – and so she should because you're so anxious to make amends you're twice the lover you were before. Never mind that you're knackered – that's the price you have to pay to still your conscience.

In adultery, truth is a luxury, lies are a necessity.

You tell yourself that an affair rejuvenates a marriage. You almost convince yourself you're doing her a favour, but a little voice at the back of your mind says 'hypocrite'.

You are never promiscuous. When it comes to liaisons you're positively picky. There are guys who claim they're reaching their century: ONE HUNDRED

WOMEN! They're lying, of course, but if what they say is even half true, it makes your own exploits seem quite tame. Mere dalliances.

Yes, when it comes to league tables you're so far down it hardly counts. Except that infidelity – even minor indiscretion – is high-maintenance. You become paranoid about anyone (especially your partner) touching your phone, your computer, your credit card bill. How do you explain dinner for two as a night you were 'late at the office dining on ham butties and crisps'?

Sometimes guilt can make you spiteful. You criticize her a lot because you want it to be HER fault that YOU strayed. You even suggest she needs to see someone about her 'moods'. '*What* moods?' she says, and you smile darkly and say, 'You know.'

She looks puzzled. She's even more puzzled when you buy her an expensive present to ease your conscience. You don't say that, of course. You just bask in the glory of being 'a generous man'.

In the end you confess. There's an absolute surge of relief as you unload and then you see her face. She's crushed but there's something else there and it takes you a moment to work out what.

She has become the WRONGED WOMAN!

You are about to be punished and you have only yourself to blame.

SHE SAYS… The sex is so wonderful that your doubts are quelled. He couldn't be like this if he was 'like *that*', surely?

You can't bring yourself to say 'unfaithful' so you call it 'it' or 'that' or 'playing away'.

In his arms you think, 'It's alright. What I have, I hold' – until one day you realize the sex is *too* frantic, *too* unselfish. He was never as good a lover before – before he needed to keep you sweet. 'Do you love me?' you say and he says 'Of course,' and inside you a little niggle blossoms because instinctively you know he's lying.

You iron his favourite shirt, knowing he will wear it to meet HER. You want to burn it clean through, but instead you iron with exquisite care. At least she doesn't get to do his shirts.

You remember all the private-eye movies you've ever seen and go through his pockets, his washing, his phone, his briefcase.

Nothing.

At first you're relieved, but then you remember how

clever he is. He does everything well, betrayal included.

And then one day you rebel. What's sauce for the goose is sauce for the gander – except that it was the gander who was at the sauce and the goose who wants to get even.

'Beauty is only sin-deep.'

You're better at it than he is. You discover your own capacity to be devious and it's HUGE. The precision with which you cover your tracks both delights and amazes you because you manage it without involving anyone, not even your best friend. This must be *your* secret: yours and the OTHER MAN's and you know he'll stay shtum because your husband is his boss.

At home you're super-careful. Emails are read, savoured and deleted. Let him pick up your phone: it's so innocent it squeaks because you delete each message after first listening. Why savour them? There'll be as many more as you choose. You are in the driving seat on this one and you like it.

You rehearse all the possible scenarios: whatever he asks, you'll be ready. You make sure there's plenty of sex but you avoid kissing him on the lips. You can only kiss one man at a time, which is strange but true.

He never had that problem, devious bastard.

Still, knowing he did it first legitimizes what you're doing now and what you're doing now is *fun*. No longer are you full-time mother, housewife, chauffeur, PA. You are an ADULTERESS – A Scarlet Woman, and you've always looked good in red.

You understand now what Bill Clinton meant when he said he did not have sexual relations with Monica Lewinsky. What you and the OM have is sex: sex impure and simple. Sexual *relations* are kept for the marital bed.

You get quite annoyed when people suggest that a women who plays away is a slapper. You're *not* a slapper. When men play away they're called 'studs'. Whatever the female equivalent of stud is, *that's* what you are.

Of course it can't last. In the end you finish the affair. For a week or two there's a space in your life. The excitement has gone and everyday existence is like salad without dressing.

You wonder if you're meant to be an adulteress. Maybe you *are* a slapper after all.

And then you find you're PREGNANT again!

The world rocks until a frantic scanning of the calendar and your diary confirms it is *not* the OM's. For a moment, when you tell him, your man is bemused. And then he smiles, as though a load has been lifted – and you know SHE'S history.

You wonder if he'll tell you one day and hope he won't. Some things are better left unsaid.

As for you, your lips are sealed.

Permanently, as any loving wife's should be.

It's easy to convince yourself you can commit adultery and there will be no consequences. You probably didn't intend it to happen. Now it has, but you are both grown up. This will be a momentary fling and then it will be over. No one else need know. No one will get hurt. Sadly, it's not that easy. One or both of you may become emotionally involved and unable to break free. Secrecy is virtually impossible. Almost inevitably someone *will* get hurt. In case that person is you or someone you care about, it would be wise to think carefully.

Rows
Arguments clear the ornaments

HE SAYS… There are forty-one known ways of conducting a row, but let's stick to the most common. First comes the silent treatment. They can hear you alright – the captain of a trawler off the Dogger Bank can hear you – they just choose not to. Requests for information are ignored or met with a violent response. Ask where your rugger shirt is and you risk it being hurled at your head. More serious requests, like 'Where's the first-aid box? I've ruptured an artery' will be met with 'Don't ask me' – which is a downright silly response as you already HAVE asked them.

Sometimes they'll recite a monologue to some mythical person within the room. 'He wants to know where the first-aid box is? Let him find out. Why should I care? Did he care when I almost fractured my ulna falling off a stepladder three years gone Easter? Did he hell! He never cares about anybody but himself …'

On and on it goes. The one thing you must *never* do is try to attract their attention by saying 'Speak to ME, please – not the wall'. This is to risk physical assault. The wisest move is to start whistling *Peter and the Wolf* while making a cat's cradle with some string. They can't stand you being gainfully employed. It throws them.

I kid you not, all women are guerrilla fighters from birth. Don't be fooled by the fragile appearance. Your average woman could repel a cruise missile if she put her mind to it. Look at history. Who burned people at the stake? Not Charles I or II; it was Elizabeth and Mary. Then you've got Boudicca and Amazons, and how do we know Attila the Hun was male? 'Attila' sounds like a feminine name to me.

*'Before you erupt, be sure it's
worth the aftershock.'*

So you see, it's in their genes.

They've had to cover it up for a century or two, now it's coming out. They're just in a domestic setting at the moment, but give them time. They'll rule the world before long.

Domestically, the 'work to rule' is one of their tried and tested methods. You sense the atmosphere has a wind-chill factor of ten so you make some innocuous remark.

'Been out today?'

'Yes.'

'Somewhere nice?'

'No.'

This is known as the Wimbledon Technique. You serve, they bat back.

'Did the weather hold up?'

'Depends what you mean by "hold-up".'

Love-fifteen to them.

'What do you want to be: part of the solution or part of the problem?'

Ask for a drop of milk, you'll get just that: a *drop*. Lunch will be a tin and an opener (with condiments if you're lucky). They know how to wound, these women. But they still set the table and put out a flower arrangement. That's to rub salt into the wound.

You say, quite nicely, 'Can I have some bread with this corned beef?' and back comes 'Please yourself'. When you realize they're not getting up for it you go yourself, but the bread bin's empty and she knew that.

Devious? Don't go there.

They're also not above a recital of your shortcomings since potty-training. The earlier ones are gleaned from your sister, who has a Judas streak a yard wide. So you get The Time You Stole the Last Kit Kat (which should have been your sibling's), The Terrible Day You Forgot to Feed the White Mice (and they ate their tails) and finally The Time You Took a Girl Out in Your Father's Car (and then it rolled back into a ditch while you were snogging).

Major crimes which, if she'd known about them, would never have let her move in with you! You are a SWINE, she concludes, and there's a pillow and some blankets in the chest on the landing.

You don't talk about it in the pub. Well, who wants to admit he's under the thumb? But it comes out, little bits here and there. That's how you know that, with some women, it gets *physical*. They jab you with a pointed finger whose tensile strength equals that of tungsten.

You, being a man, cannot retaliate.

She, being a woman, trades on this.

Ducking and weaving is the answer here, apparently, and results in no more than glancing blows. (This behaviour often produces genuine remorse on their part, I'm told, so stick it out. It will be worth it in the end).

'Two wrongs don't make a right but they make a good excuse.'

When all else fails, they bring on the waterworks.

Women can cry more easily than men because their bladder is situated nearer their eyes. They can turn the tears on and off at will and produce little heaving noises in their chest to denote extreme distress.

When men cry their eyes go piggy and unattractive. Women's eyes widen into twin pools of reproach. 'Look what you did to me, you brute!' they seem to say.

And against your will it turns you on and that's exactly what they intended. You just melt and the next minute you've said 'Sorry, sorry, sorry' although you still don't know what you've done.

I've told you, women, bless them, have no scruples.

'Weaker sex'?

I should be so lucky!

SHE SAYS… Women are, by nature, peacemakers but there are limits. I mean, *everyone* argues. You say the wrong thing, bring up the past, make a scene, throw the odd plate – that's life. But men can't seem to leave it at that. They can't just kiss and make up (which can be really cool); they *have* to have the last word.

You think you've found Mr. Right and find he's Mr. Never Wrong. Physical violence is out because the world frowns on it, so they've invented ways of fighting that don't leave a mark.

One of their little ploys is putting you in the wrong, and that can be worse than physical violence. At least you can jail them for that.

Smugness is harder to pin down.

'She's at it again,' their expression says. 'Oh, well, I'll just bear it until she decides to stop.' Beat their chest with your clenched fist and you're a madwoman. Beat your own chest in exasperation and you're a neurotic.

You can't win.

The other little foible beloved of the men in our lives is the SMIRK. You've seen it. They're caught bang to rights but they won't admit it. Instead they smirk as if to say 'Think that if you like, but you're wrong'. Scream or argue and the smirk just gets wider.

If smirking was a money-spinner, all men would be millionaires.

And the worst thing is it makes you doubt yourself. I mean, you want to believe them because you love them. You stand there thinking, 'Well, if he's right we can have a good cuddle and it'll all be lovely,' and nine times out of ten you just give in.

'Don't be right, be reasonable.'

Which is exactly the result he expected.

When women learn how to smirk we'll shatter the universe, never mind the glass ceiling.

Men's other major weapon is sarcasm. You make a few simple rules – put towels on rails, put lids back on jars – and the next minute he's goose-stepping round the kitchen, forefinger under his nostrils, shouting *'Achtung!'*

And straight away he's put you off-balance. You feel bossy, tyrannical and picky. The next time you're about to ask him to put out the trash you remember *'Achtung!'* and carry it out to the bin yourself. Which really sucks because you know he's conned you and although he's sitting with his choirboy expression in place you know he knows it, too.

Before he moved in he agreed to share the housework and he keeps his promise. A clean fifty-fifty split: he makes the messes, you clear them up.

'Even when he loves and she loves it doesn't take a genius to produce a shouting match.'

Now this should be the subject of arbitration and you're prepared to be reasonable, but does he meet you halfway? Does he hell! He sees the 'We need to talk sign' in your eyes and the next minute you're being seduced. Works every time. You lie back but you're not thinking about England; you're thinking about the remote possibility of his doing the washing-up one day.

Not that it isn't an enjoyable way of being stymied, but it's hardly fair, is it?

Men are also adept at The Loud Sigh. This is as good as the worst expletive in that it sets your nerves jangling. Repeated, it can reduce you to a jelly and he loses no opportunity to exploit it. Take more than a minute to fix your face or find your other earring and he lets out a gust. Losing your car key and having to turn your bag out on the bonnet is at least a two-sigh job – four if the key was in your pocket all the time.

They also use it if you sit on the remote control, which is the only way of stopping them channel-hopping in love scenes. They don't understand the female need to see Brad's lips actually meet Angelina's so, just as the noses touch – *Zap!* He's clicked to Sport on Four and when you scream and bite the cushions he gives one of those long, slow sighs.

GOD!

Most of all men use sighing in shops. The male sigh can trigger sprinklers on three floors of Selfridge's and all because you can't immediately choose between aqua and turquoise.

Men have got clever since we got emancipated. They can't keep you in line by societal disapproval so they use other means. One of them is forgetfulness employed as an offensive weapon. They can remember the number of their first car, their PIN and the telephone number of Moss Bros suit hire.

But the anniversary of the day you met? That's beyond their ken. Unless it happened to fall on Cup Final Day, in which case it's imprinted on their memory and that makes things worse. If you accuse them of being deliberately spiteful, you get that hurt look or else the pitying look that says you're being petty but of course you can't help it.

The real weapon, of course, is SULKING. Men imbibe the art of sulking with their mother's milk although they'll never admit it. 'Something wrong?' you ask, when they haven't spoken since Tuesday. You get a shrug or a raised eyebrow which, roughly interpreted, means 'You know very well what's wrong!' One raised eyebrow is a storm warning; two means 'Batten down the hatches'. Two eyebrows and a shrug means 'I'd leave tonight only you haven't ironed my shirts yet'.

Some sulkers will toy with their food and then push away the plate. This can go on for days but seldom results in weight loss as they sandwich cheese between digestive biscuits every time your back's turned. Sulking can really peak in bed. He turns his back, then punches his pillow into shape.

This is the equivalent of a Maori Haka.

He lies on the extreme edge of the bed but if, by accident, your limbs touch, he jumps like someone having coronary resuscitation in *ER*.

Pretend to fall asleep and he'll punch his pillow

again or clear his throat – positively anything to keep his audience awake.

Sulking *needs* an audience.

At breakfast time he'll ostentatiously spurn the tea you made and make himself a coffee, although you both know he loathes coffee in the morning. This is designed to add a dash of martyrdom and always worked with his mother.

You are made of sterner stuff.

> *'Self-pity is the enemy of reason.'*

In the end you get fed up and coax him out of it. He plays hard to get at first, pretending not to notice you're on your knees in supplication. When he does grant pardon he suddenly switches on the sun – as though he hasn't been a miserable bastard for days.

He whistles round the house, makes corny jokes and may even buy you a bunch of highly coloured chrysanths when he goes for petrol. This is known as PSAA, or Post-Sulk Arsing About, and is a very good time to ask for more housekeeping or a weekend in Torquay.

The wise woman exploits this period to the hilt. The unwise woman says, 'Decided to speak now, have we?'

Personally, I'm an exploiter.

Well, life's too short, isn't it?

Deal with it

An occasional row can clear the air, and making up afterwards can be particularly pleasant. If you are rowing often and for little or no reason, however, you need to look at the underlying relationship. Is there resentment on one side or the other? Are there stresses on the work front or within the wider family? If no such factors exist and you are both simply volatile and ready to fight at the drop of a hat, it can help to have a truce object, some ludicrous ornament which, once produced, brings with it a fifteen-minute silence. At the end of that time, hopefully there'll be nothing you wish to fight about.

Apologies
Love means always having to say you're sorry

HE SAYS… There's an immortal line: 'Love means never having to say you're sorry.' Well, immortal it may be, accurate it ain't. Any lover will tell you that grovelling – the art of saying 'Sorry' in forty-seven languages – is at the heart of any good relationship.

If you take a hard look at the seven deadly sins, the deadliest one is pride. Pride can screw up a relationship more efficiently than any other factor.

You know how it is: you've been a heel and you know it. But can you come right out and say it? Like hell you can. You *want* to. You form the words, but that something somewhere in the back of your mind says 'You'll be less of a man if you back down'.

So you say 'Please yourself' or 'If that's what you want to think'.

You know she doesn't want to think it. She's begging to be contradicted, so why can't YOU do what YOU want and say 'I'm sorry'?

Sometimes you do get something out but then you have to qualify it. 'OK, so I was a bastard not to call and let you worry – but what about that time you…?'

And you go on and on about something entirely irrelevant that should have been long forgotten.

You do that because your dignity is threatened.

I mean, does it *really* matter that you've forgotten to lift the loo seat when she's ASKED and ASKED? Women can start rows quicker than a Celtic player in the Rangers' dressing room, so why is it YOU who must back down?

The male sex isn't built to give way. There may be men who enjoy apologizing, but they must be descended from St Teresa of Avila – and she died a virgin.

> *'Saying sorry is akin to surgery.*
> *Both cause exquisite pain.'*

The first love we come across (unless we're very unlucky) is parental love. Parents love you unconditionally: the only kind of love that really counts. So it's easy to say 'Sorry, Mum,' knowing you'll get a hug and a whispered, 'Forget it. It doesn't matter.'

Saying sorry to a lover is entirely different. It's fraught with uncertainty. Admit this once that you were in the wrong and you give them a HOLD over you. Worse, they may forgive you and then follow it up with a lecture on the fifty-seven other things for which you should apologize.

When a woman thinks she has you in the apology mode she'll exploit it to the hilt.

It's easy to see that one apology as a slippery slope. Back down now and you'll be doing it forever. You'll be in the spare bedroom for Christmas and sleeping in the shed by Easter. Whoever said a husband is a lover with the backbone extracted wasn't far wrong, you tell yourself. The fact that this is the woman you love standing in front of you is forgotten. She has become the ENEMY. Bring out the cannon, man the ramparts and never, ever surrender.

'After each row there is a little
less relationship left to save.'

But once the seed of guilt is planted you weaken, so you try other ways of saying sorry. How many men have come home from a bender with a bunch of hollyhocks preceding them through the door, only to have them trashed by five feet of fury?

Doing a particularly nasty chore, however, can work wonders. 'Darling I cleaned out that blocked drain' can be effective at breaking a twenty-four-hour silence, even if all she says is that you should have thrown yourself out with the assorted gunge. At least she's *speaking*. At least you won't be sleeping back-to-back tonight and she can quit giving a little sob every time she senses you're dropping off.

What you should *never* do is issue an apology through clenched teeth. Women have radar. Your lips may say 'Sorry' but they pick up the venom behind the words. 'OK bitch: better get it over with although you don't deserve it. If I don't you'll sulk all week.' Even if you smile like a seraph they'll KNOW that's what you're thinking! I mean, all women are witches under the skin. The sooner they bring back the ducking stool the better.

In the heat of an argument, with the words rattling out like machine-gun bullets, you can go too far. At times like that it helps to get away from the scene of conflict. Go out and swear at the delphiniums. Curse the budgie. Trash the evening paper. Don't, for God's sake, take a drive round the block. You're liable to wind up round a lamppost and have to start apologizing for losing the no-claims bonus.

Above all, don't see lovemaking as the cure for all woes. Throwing sex at a simmering situation is like putting petrol on a bonfire. There may be a fractional cessation of flame but the resultant explosion will be heard at sea.

You could try going all Bohemian. Throw some pillows on the bedroom floor, light a candle, open some sangria and invite discussion. This will either produce a truce or a clip around the earhole but it's worth a try.

Scientists claim an apology has an immediate effect on your health (other than saving you from that clip round the earhole) in that it lowers your blood pressure. It also means she can quit asking the dog to ask you to pass the salt or slamming your plate in front of you with such force that gravy hits the ceiling at 45mph.

According to the psychoanalyst Engel, you should always apologize and hope your apology would be reciprocated. If it isn't, you should reflect on the nobility of your own actions rather than dwell on your lover's lack.

Well, the devil with that. Love may mean always having to say sorry, but no one can blame you if you mind like hell!

SHE SAYS… All the while you're growing up, people feed you a myth. All relationships are heterosexual, permanent, productive and gooily sentimental. The first time you throw a plate or, worse, have to duck one, the cosy world you've been promised falls apart.

Henceforth you will live in the real world and in the real world your role is to say 'Sorry'.

Most arguments are trivial. He forgot to praise your lasagne. He swore at the dog, he switched on teletext to get the soccer before he shouted 'I'm home!' It begins with a tiny flicker and ends in Cold War Mark II. If no one breaks the deadlock, it can fester for weeks.

*'Apologizing can become not so much
a habit, more a way of life.'*

But why should it have to be YOU who backs down? You didn't start it. HE started it when he was unloving.

But if you love him, shouldn't you reach out? You lie back-to-back in bed, both coiled like springs in case flesh should touch flesh. You each rehearse the olive branch, but who should be the first to offer it?

You go over it in your head, acknowledging the fact that in real life, there is no unadulterated right and wrong. Love means having to say sorry even when you aren't – and HE started it and if he had a caring bone in his body he'd be grovelling by now.

Your better self reminds you that the same thing could apply to you. You think of what a whispered apology could mean. Warm arms around you, soothing words, the best kind of sex: the healing kind. All you have to do is say one five-letter word beginning with S. But he's a hard-hearted pig who knows you'll crack first and why should you give him the satisfaction?

At times like this you want your mother, who was never unreasonable or cruel. Even your father had a charitable side. But you share a bed with an arrogant shit who will take that five-letter word as a sign of weakness and use it against you.

If *he'd* had reasonable parents he might've been different. Instead, they ruined him; now *you're* paying for it. If only he understood how much a 'sorry' would mean – but men don't understand women. They know nothing about them except that they have mammary glands.

You're winding yourself up now and all the while you know you could stop it all with one little word.

At 3am you're still wide awake and he – the ingrate, the oppressor, the hard-hearted villain – is gently snoring. You try a well-placed elbow in the ribs but he just turns over. How can he *sleep*? Because, stupid fool that he is, he thinks a bunch of gerberas bought from the garage on his way home tomorrow will break you down.

More fool him.

Alone in the 4am kitchen you examine the bleakness of a life where disagreements become arguments, arguments become rows and rows become conflicts. Of course, if you said 'Sorry' it would all be over. You say it aloud in the silence. 'Sorry. I love you. Let's never fight again.' After all, he is not only your lover, he's your best friend, the one who rubs your back when you have period pain and even loves you with Velcros in…

At this point you seize a pan-scrubber and attack the ingrained dirt around the hotplates. What did your mother tell you? 'Never let the sun go down on an argument.' Why didn't someone tell *him* that? For a moment you contemplate carrying the washing-up bowl into the bedroom and dowsing him with suds.

Except that wouldn't be loving. Love is gentle, complicated, sad and terrifying. What it is *not* is silent.

If this be love let it speak its name. For a moment you wonder if you read that somewhere or if you made it up. If the latter, you are cleverer than you thought. Profound, even. And practical, too, because the hotplate is gleaming.

In the bedroom he lies, a black hulk in the light from the open door. 'Are you awake?' For a terrible moment there's no answer and then the hulk changes shape, morphs into open arms. 'I'm sorry.'

'Me, too.'

'It was my fault.'

'No, mine.'

'There you go again! You always have to be right!'

Then two voices say: 'I don't believe you sometimes!'

Suddenly you're laughing and he is, too, and it's going to be alright.

Deal with it

Whoever said 'Never explain, never apologize' didn't understand co-existence. Sometimes apologies, however hard to make, are necessary. Occasionally, even when they're undeserved, they're advisable. Don't make them simply to produce peace; that seldom works because you'll harbour resentment. But if you make a considered decision to apologize, don't see it as weakness. Restoring harmony with a thoughtful apology is an act of strength. Why continue in a state of siege when one word – a simple 'Sorry' – could end it all? Pride is a cold bedfellow, especially when that same five-letter word may be trembling on your partner's lips.

Breaking Up
They said it would never work – and they were right

HE SAYS… In every man's life there comes a moment when you're dumped. Sometimes they simply don't turn up, and that can be agony. You sit there trying to look at your watch without anyone seeing, telling yourself that if you count up to ten she'll walk through the door, running through all the things that could have happened to hold her up, checking that your phone is on because surely she'll ring to explain.

It's forty-five minutes before you give up and chalk it down to experience. You console yourself by thinking no one need know. You might even tell everyone *you* were the one who failed to show – except that her best friend tells your best friend and you get the sympathy vote. If that happens a couple of times it makes you paranoid.

You don't make dates because what's the point? You start examining yourself in mirrors, asking 'why you?' You're an OK bloke: not handsome but not hideous. You brush your teeth, your nails are clean, you make sure your breath is lemon-fresh.

And still the heave-ho.

And then one day she is there and she's the best of them all. Not only gorgeous but trustworthy. Within weeks you're living together and rejection is no longer part of your vocabulary.

The moment when you realize it isn't working can creep up on you. By rights, it should come like a thunderclap, but no: you hear a note in her voice that wasn't there before. A tinge of resentment that reminds you of the playground. 'I'm not going to play any more if you're going to be like *that*.'

Except that this isn't the playground and you've done nothing wrong.

The next day it's there again. She's picking on you: you're too loud, too silent, too lazy, too interfering.

In other words, you can't win.

And then she says the fatal words: 'Mum thinks…'

Well, frankly, it's not up to her mother to think anything. It's her *daughter* you're shagging, not her – and, yes, that's coarse, but it's also true.

You have a row and Mummy Dearest is right there at the heart of it. But the making up is wonderful and for forty-eight hours it's like it was at the beginning. Blissful!

And then it's there again, the 'You've got me in your bed, what more do you want?' note. And there's another row and another making up. You even discuss having a baby but, thank God, reason prevails.

The fourth row (or maybe the fifth?) does it.

'I won't stay another night under the same roof as you!' she says, and you bite. 'That's right: run back to mother! That's where you belong.'

And just for a minute you mean it.

She can bloody well go.

'Don't leave in a huff, leave in a taxi.'

When she rings for a taxi and puts her key on the hall table you want to say 'Don't be silly' – but what's the point? You're back on the street corner, waiting, hoping and knowing in your heart that she won't be coming.

You find yourself strangely reluctant to go home. You walk across the city at night, watching TV in shop windows, gazing at your own reflection in the glass, staring into lighted rooms where everyone seems to be making love.

For some reason this brings a lump to your throat.

You look up her mother's number in your memory

bank but your fingers won't punch out the last two digits. If only you could understand *why* she went. She couldn't wait to get away from home before. Why should it be different now?

You find yourself jumping when the phone rings, but it's always someone wanting to sell you something or make up a four for squash.

You take a few days off and hibernate. You drink, but you don't eat or wash. Stubble seems to become you; you look gaunt and distinctly heavy-eyed.

Which is actually rather attractive.

'Highwaymen wanted your money or your life. Women want both.'

The girl in the flat downstairs sees you putting out the trash and does a double-take. This does you good. You can still pull. You make yourself a mound of fried eggs and Spam – the only food in the house – and spend the rest of the day swallowing milk of magnesia. Four eggs and a tin of Spam: what kind of stock-cupboard is *that*? You're considering suing for neglect until you remember your own selfishness.

What did YOU ever do to help around the house?

You're feeling remorseful when she rings.

'Zoë? How are you?'

'Fine. You?'

You subside into a chair. This is going to be a long conversation because you have no intention of giving in straight away. She wants to come back? Well, she can, but she has to learn a few lessons first.

That's when she drops the bombshell. She wants the bedside lamp and the juicer and the swivel chair and the folding table.

'Why not take the lot?' you say, in what are meant to be sarcastic tones.

She takes it quite literally. 'Oh, no need for that. You can keep the settee – and the *scales*,' she says because she and you both know YOU'RE the one who puts weight on.

So you tell her you'll leave the key downstairs and can she take everything in one go because you don't want people traipsing in and out of your home. You put just the right emphasis on those last words.

You're not the kid waiting on the street corner any more. You're a solid citizen.

But the flat's not the same when she's filleted it. She

leaves you a cactus in a blue pot and you can't make up your mind whether it's a peace offering or a message.

You drink every drop of booze in the house – even the Madeira that was for your mother's birthday – but it doesn't help. You go back to work, but that doesn't help either. The boss tells you to 'snap out of it' and the lads give you the 'more fish in the sea' routine.

One of the clerks brings you a bag of homemade drop scones and clucks sympathetically. 'Never mind' she says. 'You need taking out of yourself. My niece was dumped and she's doing phrenology at night school. There're some lovely girls on her course.'

This is accompanied with a poke in the ribs. You sit munching drop scones and contemplate a future packed with thrilling phrenology classes. When you find out what it is, you might enrol.

That night you lie in bed feeling OLD. You can see the future and it's not a pretty sight. You'll be one of those crusty old bachelors with dry skin on the backs of their hands and smelly trousers.

The prospect frightens you so much that as soon as it's a decent hour you ring home.

'Mum? No, nothing wrong. I was just thinking, I might move back in for a bit – if that's alright with you?'

SHE SAYS… It constantly amazes me that people will put up with such crummy relationships. You'd take back an orange if, on peeling, it turned out to be a lemon.

When a great romance begins to resemble the Valentine's Day Massacre do lovers turn and flee? Do they heck! They stay on, inflicting or enduring wounds while mouthing phrases like 'He's lovely when he's sober'.

So – inspect the goods, I say, and if they're not up to scratch, move on.

All the same, the moment when it's over can be terrifying. Yesterday you knew him for the swine he was; now all you can think of is that day when he brought you roses. The fact that foreplay to him meant taking off his socks is no longer relevant. You MISS him.

> *'One day you'll look back on this*
> *and it will still make you cry.'*

You crawl into the still-warm bed and try to inhale him from his pillow. You put out a tentative foot hoping against hope it will encounter warm flesh. When it doesn't, you cry until your nose runs.

Why did you let him go?

You finish his last two Four Xs because it's the only booze in the pad, forgetting that the very smell of it on his breath made you nauseous. Passionate sex scenes replay against your eyelids: not the usual coming together, during which he tried to find Sky Sport on the remote control while stimulating your nipples with his other hand. No, this is the full-blooded, no-holds-barred sex you'll have when he crawls back. The kind where *you're* on top. Never mind that he actually preferred *Match of the Day*. Next time will be different.

'If you know of a better hole, go to it.'

When he doesn't crawl back, you forswear food. Who wants to eat when hope has died? Well, if you're an ectomorph, that is. If you're a mesomorph you comfort-eat: jelly, gefilte fish, sago pudding, pound bars of whole nut (50% extra) – never mind the quality, feel the *width*.

And you phone: anyone and everyone who will listen to what a bastard he was. You're amazed and a little offended when your girlfriends tell you they knew it all along and thank God you've come to your senses. You imagine yourself on *Trisha* or *Oprah*. Your grief is touching and an agent signs you up.

OK. After three days of fasting or feasting and doing daytime telly in your head, your friends won't pick up when you call, colleagues can't cover for you any longer and you realize you need a bath.

Almost against your will you are moving into rehab.

You shower and step on the scales, convinced you've lost a stone. The needle hovers reassuringly a pound or two up on last time and your face, when you clean the steamed-up mirror, looks pink and fresh.

So you haven't died of grief.

That's when you remember that poem, the one that goes 'Love is to man a thing apart, 'tis woman's whole existence'. That was it, of course! He *didn't deserve* you!

And suddenly you realize you're free. OK, you were dumped, but you are going to rise above it. Nobility will shine from your countenance. Coachloads will come to see you thrive. You'll look more interesting because you've suffered (how cool is *that?*).

And it's not really a case of your having 'failed'. It's simply that HE failed to recognize his luck.

As you pour another drink you know the trick is to work out not what you've lost but what you've gained.

Never again will you have to watch a goal replayed until you can count the scorer's nasal hairs. The enigma of the disappearing sock is no longer your problem. The hours you spent plucking, varnishing, moisturizing just for him are now yours to use creatively. You can wear winceyette nighties and let your tummy droop.

And there'll be PARTIES! Parties, parties and more parties. You rush to the wardrobe to pick out some frocks.

It's better to have loved and lost than to have loved and lost and kept on loving.

This euphoria lasts a week. Two weeks tops. No one has a party and if they do, everyone's entwined with someone else. You live on meals for one and drink from the bottle. There's no one to rub your feet or put out the trash.

By day twelve you're talking to yourself.

You make enquiries about counselling, go on Atkins and try a new body spray. No one sniffs it like Bisto and follows you home. You find yourself playing Patience and phoning Battersea about a dog.

And then, unexpectedly, you pull and the whole darn thing begins again.

Deal with it

Sometimes relationships simply come to an end. No one has failed, no one is to blame, it is simply the natural end of something which once was splendid but now has run out of steam. It's easy to feel you have failed or to blame your partner. Regrets pile up. If only you had done, said, understood more, all would have been well. Although you may not see it at the time, this is a door closing on failure and opening to opportunity. Don't look back through rose-tinted spectacles; remember the rows as well as the love-ins. Try to be civilized about the parting and, if you feel aggrieved, remember that being happier without a partner than you were with one is the greatest revenge of all.

Exes
Feel the fear and forget it

HE SAYS… Nothing cuts a man's legs from under him as completely as stepping into another man's shoes. The peril is not apparent at first. If it was obvious, it would never happen, would it?

The truth is that women are more skilful at concealing their wounds. They don't sit around at parties gazing mournfully into their beer in the hope that something nubile will take pity on them. Their response to being dumped is to flaunt themselves. You, poor sod, see this multifaceted, infinitely desirable, out-for-fun creature and you FALL.

FALL is the operative word, because now you're in an elephant trap with slimy twelve-foot walls and her ex grinning triumphantly from above.

At first, she responds with fervour to your every move. And the sex is *fantasmaglorious*. The first time.

The second time she says would you hang on a moment. She's not sure and would you give her time to think. You suggest a short time-out (like five minutes) but she says you don't understand. She has been HURT and doesn't want to be HURT again.

You say 'That's alright, then' because you have no intention of hurting anyone. You just want to get on with IT, which is, after all, *the* most important thing in the universe at this moment.

She looks reproachful at that and you feel like a sex-maniac devoid of finer feelings.

'It's here,' she says, laying her hand on her bosom, which is the best one you've seen since Britney Spears live at the Albert Hall. She removes your hand when it joins hers and urges you to be more cerebral. This is Napoleonic Code for 'Not tonight, Josephine' so you fetch two more beers from the fridge.

'Hindsight is never 20/20.'

You get the whole story then. How she never looked at anyone else, waited on him hand and foot, even passed up an opportunity to audition for *Blue Peter*. Now he's gone and she's not sure she can let herself CARE again in case all men are the same.

You point out that you're not in the least like him.

She looks thoughtful and says 'No, HE was a Cambridge rugger blue'.

You decide not to tell her you won the egg-and-spoon in primary school and long-held doubts about the size of your genitalia resurface.

'So what DO you want?' you ask at last, in a genuine attempt to find out what's to be done.

She shakes her head and her eyes fill.

This is when you realize women think in circles. This guy is the biggest heel since Judas Iscariot, but she can't get over him. You have serious doubts about her sanity but promise to be patient and take her home in a taxi because by now you're too pissed to drive.

'Don't fight the past – cultivate the future.'

The following day you drink *a lot* of coffee. You also alternate between the 'other fish in the sea' thought and remembering how it felt when she was looking soulful and you touched her boobs. You're so carried away by this thought that the coffee you're holding tips into your lap and the whole office is transfixed by your scream.

You change your trousers and reflect that you're meeting her that night and for once you're not looking forward to it. Perhaps this one is too much trouble.

And yet…

You wish some MP would pass a law allowing a man to shoot his predecessor without fear of prison. That not being likely in the current parliament, you ring a bloke you know who was at Cambridge. You hope to be told you are taking over from the pits of the world – an idea which makes you think of John McEnroe, but she would never have gone out with a man in a headband, would she?

Your friend is a mine of information.

'Greg? Great guy. Popular with both sexes. Generous to a fault. What a scrum-half! Destined for great things'.

You put down the phone before he can give you more sickly details and go to meet her feeling as though you could walk under a duck without scratching its belly. She smiles when she sees you, but you tell yourself not to read too much into it and suggest a most expensive restaurant. That's when you break out in a sweat in case your card bounces, but mercifully she says she'd rather eat in and who needs food anyway?

She can't wait to get you into bed and you just manage to get your socks off before she pounces. Afterwards you reflect that men may be from Mars but surely women are from Broadmoor.

This woman has more facets than a Rubik's Cube and who wants to go through life trying to master a piece of plastic? You start to compose a farewell speech.

That's when she makes you Welsh rarebit with lots of mustard, just like your dad used to make when your mum threw a wobbly. You feel euphoric as you scoff it sitting up in bed, trying not to let big crumbs reach places with nerve endings. She seems to enjoy cheese on toast, too – until she sighs and says she wishes she didn't feel so mixed up.

If Greg didn't exist she could be happy with you. She thought doing sex might fix it but it hasn't. For a moment, you contemplate throwing aside the plate, crumbs and all, and taking her by force like real men do in movies.

But you are not a real man. You are a poor substitute for the only man she will ever love.

At this moment you have two choices. You can learn to live for the moment while hoping for the best. Or, like all the best reporters, you can make your excuses and leave.

Reluctantly, but now fearful of your own sanity, you opt for the latter. Outside there's a faint drizzle. You turn up your collar and begin the long walk home.

SHE SAYS... Love may be lovelier the second time around, but easier it ain't.

It begins well. You see a wicked guy gazing mournfully into his drink and immediately you're reminded of River Phoenix in that film – the one where he's saved from suicide by 'thingy', the actress who never made another picture. 'Who's the gloomy guy?' you ask your host – doing it SO casually that every eye in the room swivels, every ear cocks.

'Who? Him? Oh, that's just Ben. He's OK. Just split up with Simone. Best thing, really. They were never suited.'

'Coming second is a state of mind.'

Deep within your 36DD something stirs. When you were a little girl you had a nurse's outfit and put cold compresses on everything that couldn't run away. Now you take up your lamp and glide down the ward towards him, the theme to *The English Patient* ringing in your ears.

He looks up and it all begins.

I say 'all' because you're not just beginning a relationship with him; you're entering into a relationship with HER. You'll come to know her intimately. You'll fear her, loathe her and wish her dead – unless she *is* dead, of course, in which case you'll feel GUILTY.

None of this is apparent at first. At first you're Juliet Binoche and he's Ralph Fiennes, only this time no one's going to die. You'll heal his wounds with tact, sympathy and endless, endless sex.

And that's how it is at first.

In between steamy sessions you list your triumphs. First time he smiles, laughs, first mentions HER in derogatory tones. And the sex really is fabulous. He's been in a desert and you are his oasis. You feel a little uneasy that SHE chose the curtains but you can live with them until you move in and it's your turn.

'What's left for me?'

Life's pretty sweet – until you find her tampons in his bathroom cabinet and cry for half an hour while he taps on the door and asks if everything is alright. You cry because what you can't bear is the thought of intimacy – *his* intimacy – with anyone else but you. And tampons are as intimate as it gets.

From now on HE will be your secondary consideration. SHE obsesses you, to the extent that you lurk outside the place where she works just to see her in the flesh. At first sight she is reassuring. She's at least seven pounds overweight, her stockings are wrinkled at the ankles and her roots are showing.

On second thoughts, this depresses you. She is so secure in her womanliness, so triumphantly *female*, that little things like roots and love handles are matterless. The fact is he wanted HER, warts and all. You must pluck and tint and cover up your lumpy thighs. If YOU went he wouldn't even notice.

Around about now he asks why every conversation seems to come round to HER.

He sounds irritated and this increases your insecurity. He can't bear to talk about HER. YOU annoy him. You want to ask 'Was it better with her?' but you don't dare. Forbidden to discuss, you resort to subterfuge. While he fetches a double tikka marsala you go through his photographs. In every picture of them together he is smiling.

How often does he smile with YOU?

You're up to two when he returns and wants to know why his desk is half-open with photographs hanging out. You cry, the tikka marsala goes cold and when you go to bed he says *non possibile*. You sit up all night in the bathroom with the door closed and the light on. A prolonged search reveals a false eyelash under the sink, a rusty Ladyshave and a pair of La Perla panties, size 8-10, which gives the lie to your theory that she's a 16-18.

Next day you go on a diet and vow never to eat tikka marsala again. He sees your swollen eyes but his only response is to roll his own.

On the second day of your diet you confide in your best friend. She's mildly sympathetic but points out that possession is nine-tenths of the law.

'Enjoy!' she says with a shrug, and you ask yourself why you never realized how bloody superficial she is. When she suggests lunch you remind her you're on a diet and hint that a true best friend would have remembered that.

Starvation makes you waif-like, which increases your confidence and you get through two whole days of fasting and not mentioning HER when you see HIM. You spray his bathroom end to end with room freshener until you have to gasp for breath. A vision of HER being wafted out of the open window on a tide of Spring Meadow is so satisfying that you have to sit down on the loo to savour it.

That night he says his sister has a birthday coming

up and would you like to meet his family? You want to ask if he ever took HER home, but wisdom prevails.

That night you have the kind of sex only possible when exes are banished from the bed. Post-orgasm you realize that possession IS nine-tenths of the law and resolve to give your reinstated best friend that Donna Karan top she always coveted.

The next morning you don't feel the need to cover your cellulite as you pad to the loo and you leave your deodorant in his bathroom cabinet.

A little thing, but important nevertheless.

Deal with it

Second-time-around comes complete with baggage. That is inevitable. If you are supremely confident, you accept all the relationship has to offer and rise above the drawbacks. If you are at all insecure, the thought that you are walking in someone else's footsteps can bring you down. Remember *you* were chosen for yourself – not as a substitute. What you have together is alive; the only thing that can spoil it is allowing the past to intrude. That past is dead and has only the power you choose to give to it.

Living Together
Home is where you go when the pubs shut

HE SAYS…Most women want to look after you. It's an inbuilt thing, the cherishing gene. Comes of being mothers, or potential mothers, I suppose.

The drawback is that they have to *possess* you. They like to know where you are, what time you'll be back; they fill every minute with activity: her family, your family, shopping, going to friends, having friends back, shopping, painting and decorating, shopping.

They make lists of things that must be done and tick them off. In order to breathe, you have to invent things: work trips, dental appointments. I've had forty-seven fillings in the last three years unless you look in my mouth. And once you start lying it's the beginning of the end.

But the male/female relationship is essentially the triumph of hope over experience. You swear you'll never shack up with anyone again. You fret a bit in case sexual frustration will send you doolally, but there are always one-night stands.

Anything's better than moving in. You'll never do *that* again – except that you do. You get tired of leaving a warm bed at 2am or setting her alarm for six so you can get a change of clothing before you go to work and it just seems natural to move in together. Neither of you think too much about the future. We're the NOW generation, aren't we? 'Live now, worry later.'

Anyway, there you are, either side of a table and a bit self-conscious. In bed you feel comfortable; it's the *table* that's intimidating. You can't make small talk day in, day out and you don't know one another well enough for silence yet. She hides things from you – tampons, her razor – and that's nice. The last one let it all hang out, which was exciting at first but then it got embarrassing.

'Happy co-existence requires that
you ignore some facts.'

It's not all plain sailing, of course. You have arguments over money because you're both used to making your own decisions. And she has this thing about greens. You've managed to live for years without a sprout passing your lips; she thinks they're the elixir of life.

But apart from that, she gives you space. She's funny really – good company. Her mother's a bit of a pain, but so is yours. They don't mean it. It's just years and years of nagging you to wash your neck. They get into the habit.

Anyway, you rub along together quite nicely. Your friends like her. Her friends are OK with you. They make little digs now and then about when's the big day but you can handle that.

Women are like that about weddings.

I mean, the average stag night is really a wake. We make a noise but we know we're saying goodbye to freedom. Not so with hen nights! Pure, unalloyed celebration. They are over the moon at the prospect of losing their freedom. 'Tie me down. Please, please, please! The sooner the better.'

I can't explain the difference but I know it's there.

'Don't panic! Heaven is not reached in a single bound.'

At times you think about the future. You both want children. You talk about it, but CAREFULLY. In the abstract. Not 'WE will have a baby one day'. It's always 'I would like a child eventually' with the emphasis on the 'I'.

You're careful about what you say to other people, too. If they ask if you're married, you say 'No' quite firmly and then you say 'There is someone but it's not OFFICIAL.'

That's the word to avoid.

I know women pay their own way nowadays, but there's still that feeling that a married man's responsible. And who wants to be responsible for another human being when they're handing redundancies out like jelly beans?

So you tell yourself that nothing's forever. One day it'll be over. You'll do it decently but in the end you'll go.

You go on thinking like that and then one day, one ordinary Sunday, it comes over you that this is IT. You wait to be spooked. You're in IT which is spelled J-A-I-L but you're not scared.

She's just laughing and going on about something. Not anything important and somehow that's what you want: just to be ordinary like this for the rest of time as long as it's with her. By rights there ought to be violins but there's just some crass ad on the telly going on about how women shouldn't let incontinence hold them back.

For a moment you wonder if she'll ever need incontinence pads and will you still love her if she does?

And somehow you know that if ever that day comes, you will.

SHE SAYS… OK, you got your fingers burned and never, ever again will you share a roof with a man. ANY man! Men fart, moon, have hordes of objectionable mates and cut their toenails in the living room. Oddly, you can't remember your father being that objectionable but how much do children really know about what goes on inside a marriage?

Your folks seem serene enough now, and your mother hasn't been put off because she keeps throwing out hints about you getting long in the tooth and how nice all her friend's grandchildren are.

Her favourite phrase is 'settling down' and it's such a downer. Who wants to 'settle down'? It sounds like a cake you've taken out of the oven too soon.

You're not cut out for living in tandem. You have a good social life, work is stimulating and it's nice to travel alone because you only have to cater to your own needs. You have three holidays in the twelve months after the split. One is work but the others are bliss: lazy, sunlit days with the scents of Africa drifting off the water and wine as cheap as chips.

Your future is rosy. You will work hard and play hard. There will be men but they will be transients: creatures who pass in the night. *One* night.

The flat fills up with travel brochures and you can hardly wait to get home each night. Norway in the spring or Vientiane in autumn. Decisions, decisions.

And then you meet HIM! He's funny, warm, and intelligent so you try to cool it. You even go so far as printing in large bold letters 'DO NOT GO THERE' and sticking it on the door of the fridge.

Two months later he moves in while you're still trying to work out how you could have been so monumentally stupid to get into this position.

'Men have a distinct advantage. They marry later and die earlier.'

The sex is wonderful, he pulls his weight in the house, you LIKE him – but still you're scared. It will end in tears. He will get on your nerves or you will get on his or his mates will be round every night or he won't pay his share.

You junk the travel brochures to make room but you keep a few in the bathroom and they're your insurance. When it all goes wrong, you'll take off. Provence, maybe, or the Algarve.

The first row is over nothing. He doesn't say it but you know he's thinking that you deliberately picked a fight. And it's true. It's almost as though you're saying 'See, I'm a nasty bitch so why not go now?'

I mean, what he did was *nothing*. Unpacking the supermarket shop, he put raw meat on the top shelf in the fridge and it dripped down and you went ape-shit. He stays calm and you can't help admiring him.

'Living together is no more natural to humans
than a cage is to a chimpanzee. On the other
hand, if you want three meals a day...'

And that's it.

No sniping, no sulking and none of the ghastly 'No hard feelings' stuff either. In the loo, clutching Norway and the fjords for comfort, you face the fact that this one is GROWN-UP. You can deal with boys. Adults are more complicated.

The worst of it is you can't confide in anyone. Your friends adore him. Even your dad has indicated grudging approval. You want someone to listen to all the good reasons why you're not ready to settle down and even if you were, he's not the right man.

You contemplate ringing a helpline. 'Hello. I'm sorry to bother you, but things are going so well I'm bricking it.' What would a counsellor say to *that*?

You know what your mum's sister would say. 'She's always been contrary. She doesn't get it from our side.' And perhaps you *are* contrary. Any other woman would be down on her knees giving thanks.

When he goes to Birmingham for a week you expect to be relieved, but you miss him. You make a meal for his first night home and even do pudding. He asks for seconds and says it's cordon bleu. It's all quite ordinary. Humdrum, even. No moonlit night. No scent of Africa on the water. Just a nice feeling.

He smiles again and gets up to make the coffee and as you watch him, you realize something has happened.

You feel different.

Perhaps this is what they mean when they talk about 'settling down'. If it is, it's not as bad as you thought it would be.

Are you 'in love'? How do you tell? You're happy and that's enough for now.

Deal with it

If you've thought it through, the moment you move in together shouldn't hold too many fears. Don't feel you have to 'begin as you mean to go on'. It takes time to find the pattern of living that's comfortable for you both. If possible move into a new place, especially if the old places hold memories. If a move isn't possible, whoever was there first should surrender occupation rights so that you both start from an equal footing. Don't feel you must assume an aggressively male or female role – Tarzan in the treetops, Jane tending the campfire. You each managed perfectly well on your own. Now you must gradually blend your lifestyles until they are one. No need to hurry. Hopefully, you have the rest of your life to get it right.

Family
God sends you friends, the Inquisition sends you relations

HE SAYS... When you're a kid the family is your snuggle blanket. It tucks around you, shields you, protects you, gives you a kick up the bum when you need it.

Later on you go through a phase where it's a millstone. It hates you, you hate them, you can't wait to get away. But deep down, even in the eyeball-to-eyeball confrontations, you know they're there for you. You swim in the same gene pool, how else could it be?

A lovely phase follows, one where you have your own space but go home for high days and holidays. That's a good time: the moment when you understand all that nagging, all those sacrifices, all the reasons why your kid brother is not the obnoxious brat you thought he was, or your big sister is not an overbearing nun, she's actually all right and woe betide any guy who mistreats her.

And then you fall in love.

Love, as you know, reduces your faculties to stand-by mode. All you want is to be with THE ONE. To achieve that, you will pay any price, do any deed, carry any load. Even her family.

You know your loved one's mother doesn't like you when she introduces you as 'my daughter's first fiancée'. So *that's* the way it is, you think, but do you speak up? Not if you've got sense, you don't.

If you are going to survive in the jungle known as 'the in-laws' the first rule is 'never retaliate'. Whether or not you're going in for the bit of paper, you are pledging to put up with better or worse, richer or poorer, sickness or health.

> *'Your family is a corset.*
> *HERS is a strait-jacket.'*

Cats don't marry, but they have the right idea about families. Your average cat submits to family life only at feeding times or when the temperature outside is zero and it needs the fire. The rest of the time it opts out.

Sadly, what is allowable in the animal kingdom is not on offer for humans.

Once you are 'one of us' you are a moth in a Venus fly-trap. Around you sit the jury: her parents, aunts, siblings, cousins, grandparents, godparents and every other damn parent you can think of. They pass judgement and believe me, 'Not guilty' is not an option.

If you do housework you're a pansy. If you don't, you're a selfish slob. Slave away to earn promotion: you're 'neglecting her'. Work at a moderate pace and you're a 'good-for-nothing bum'. If you cry when the dog dies, you're a wimp; if you don't, you're an insensitive bastard. If you make a decision without consulting her, you're arrogant – but she can decide you're moving to Nova Scotia and if you demur you're Hannibal Lecter. Ask her to come to a football match with you and you're 'clingy'; go with the boys and you're 'refusing to grow up'.

She doesn't think these things. She's OK with the way you are – until *they* gang up on her. 'Darling, do you think you could be just a teeny bit more tactful with mum, Aunt Agatha, brother, cousin once removed?' Face it, it will be golden wedding time before you will wield the same influence as the people she bonded with at birth.

Family occasions are the moment you realize that what couldn't get worse is defying the Law of Nature and worsening before your very eyes. Christmas should be the apex of the year; too often it's the nadir.

But you love the woman. You can cope.

By the end of the evening you have cultivated one parent, one aunt, four cousins and her second cousin's idiot child who put its tongue out at you and then accused you, at the top of its treble, of giving it a dirty look. Instead of crennelating its little ears you read aloud to it from a *Bob the Builder* book. You even do actions. And it works. They beam approvingly because you are 'fitting in'.

Fitting in is Family Law, which is equivalent to Holy Writ and cannot be gainsaid.

When you set up home with a woman, you have this vision of a love nest: you and her in a rose-covered cottage and the door firmly shut against the outside world. When she had keys cut for every family member 'just in case', you felt a little frisson of unease. You had to grit your teeth as your love nest became Piccadilly Circus, with family members coming and going round the clock.

Alone in the loo you asked God to give you just twenty-four hours without hearing someone calling 'Only me!' as they waltz through your front door, but as you already suspected, God is either dead or deaf and ignores your plea. So they drank your gin and used all your hot water just when you wanted a shower, and then the thing you dreaded most happened: her sister's marital discord, and she threatened to leave home and move in with you.

> *'The family, for all its splendour, can be the source of what ails us.'*

You went so far as to get a list of B&Bs – good places, half of them round the corner. But 'family' can't exist in B&B. 'Family' have to share your bed with your woman while you sleep on the sofa – not that that matters because you can't have sex with family in the house. But *mi casa, su casa* is lettered through your beloved like Blackpool is through rock – and that's one of the reasons why you love her.

Even when they don't split up they ring at midnight to say they're out of bread or flour or kitchen roll and you have to drive to the all-night garage to stock up for them because, after all, they're 'family'. Then there's anniversaries, the 142 family occasions you have to remember. She plays this silly game. 'Now whose birthday will it be next week?' and woe betide you if you guess wrong.

That's why women can't understand the rules of sport: whole areas of their brain are given over to remembering second cousin Lily's anniversary and sending the appropriate card.

Half the trouble with families is that newcomers are expected to know the rules. Your own family may have talked non-stop, nothing held back. You fall in love and the new bunch are Trappist monks. The first time you start on about anything in the least sensitive they look like hens that haven't laid for weeks.

And the reverse is true. If your family knew a decent silence when they saw it and you join up with gas bags, you're in trouble. They'll call you 'deep' or 'moody'. They'll decide you're hiding something or are secretly despising them. The one thing they won't call you is decently reticent.

No, face it, chaps: when you join up with a family there's only one option open to you. Swallow the pill, drink the draught, bare your chest to the knife.

There's no escape.

It's the price you pay for love. And actually, it opens your eyes. You come back from one of 'their' occasions and you pick up the phone. 'It's me, Mum. Oh, nothing special. I was just thinking about you.'

Your family doesn't go in for words like 'gratitude' or 'love' but she knows what you're thinking. Of course she does. She shares your genes.

'Horatius may have kept the bridge but even he couldn't manage his mother-in-law.'

SHE SAYS... God sends you friends, the Inquisition picks your family. That profound thought occurs to you around your early teens. Survive eighteen years with the average family and you can stick anything. Sisters pinch your best clothes, brothers expect you to wait on them and we all know what parents do. Philip Larkin made sure of that.

You grow up consoled by only one thought: one day you'll be FREE. No more family Christmases, first communions, bar mitzvahs or other assorted occasions. You will be the cat that walks alone. And you are. For what seems like five minutes.

Then the *other* family looms up. HIS family. YOUR family now. For better or worse and guess which one it's going to be?

You become the rope in a tug-of-war. On one side is his mother, who wants her darling boy all to herself and if he wants you, so-be-it. On the other side is your family, who understandably don't want to lose you.

A bidding war breaks out. His mother offers to buy a sofa. When your mother hears that, she offers to buy *two* sofas. Three months later they no longer speak and you have to use ropes to swing from room to room, so closely packed is the furniture and assorted bric-à-brac.

> *'Most families have a closet just*
> *bursting with skeletons.'*

This is when you realize that 'your own home' is just a euphemism for a war zone: hotly contested territory for two feuding families to fight over.

Then there're family 'do's'. Your lot ate out at a fancy restaurant. His lot 'bake'. Quiches, pies, salads, trifles, upside-down cake and not forgetting Aunty Mabel's apple slice, which has bits of cat's hair sticking to the pastry and has to be eaten as part of the family ritual. Do's in his family usually end up in a row. Uncle

George is a quiet drunk; Uncle Bob an obstreperous one. The women go at one another like Kilkenny cats and you have to decide which side you're on – which really makes solving the Arab/Israeli conflict look like a doddle.

You're also getting two streams of advice. Your mum says you should live a little before you start a family. His mum is reduced to making rocking motions with her arms whenever she lays eyes on you. Let your tummy sag for a second and hope springs up in her eyes. You begin to feel like an incubator and it's not a nice feeling.

But somehow you find yourself adjusting to 'being one of us'. You mind less and less when they suggest you get net curtains or warn you not to keep mushrooms in the fridge. Your windows stay defiantly bare and the mushrooms remain *in situ* but you've learned to ride with the punches.

And something else has happened.

You begin to realize that your own family wasn't as constricting as you thought they were. At least they never rang at 12.15 because they hadn't heard from you all day. They didn't want to insure your life or persuade you to go shares in a lottery syndicate. You ask God to forgive you for hating your siblings and thank Him for preventing you from smashing this new lot in the mouth.

There's a family occasion of one sort or another every week, or so it seems, and you're on the baking rota. You find yourself buying stuff at M&S and distressing it a bit so you can pass it off as yours, and you rather resent the fact that this lot have turned you into a cheat. You also remember the times your own mum tried to teach you the basics of the Victoria sponge and you told her cooking was for the birds. Now when she rings to tell you it's time to put on the thicker duvet, you're more inclined to listen.

'Parents want to find out what you're doing – and stop you doing it.'

Mums *do* know something.

Envy fills you at the ease with which your man can adapt to your presence. Not just his certainty that you will change the bed, buy the groceries, weed the window-box. From the moment you became his mate, he blanked all his family's birthdays or other special occasions.

Now it's up to YOU to remember them, buy the card, write it and post it, together with the gift you have purchased if appropriate. By making them 'your family', he has neatly sidestepped their being 'his family' – at least when it comes to hard work.

There are compensations, of course – not least that you can have carnal relations with one particular family member, who is serially gorgeous even if he won't remember birthdays.

And then there's always someone to ring when the computer won't work or the dog has fleas. That family has experts on every disorder known to man – including a few man hasn't thought of yet.

Eventually, even in your worst moments, you manage to remember that if it hadn't been for this lot (or more particularly his mother) you'd never have met him – and he *does* look lovely in the morning when he's only half-awake.

Besides, if you don't submit to family life, all you have to look forward to is the menopause, going bald on top while sprouting facial hair, losing your marbles and ending up in a home.

There's no decision to make, is there?

Deal with it

Like them or loathe them, there's no escaping them. Once you accept that however much you might wish it they will not disappear, you can set about seeing what must be endured, what can be enjoyed and what can be changed. Affection compensates for much within your own family; in-laws do not come with that degree of familiarity. Make allowances for differences in upbringing and try to understand their code, even if you will never make it your own. When you have done your best to accommodate them, allow things to flow over you. They matter, but not as much as the nuclear family, of which you and your lover are part.

Babies
Something to do when there's nothing on telly

HE SAYS…Forget earthquakes, meteorites, avian flu or STDs. The greatest threat facing man is the biological clock.

HERS, that is, not yours.

Until now she's seemed totally undomesticated, let alone broody. This is a woman who thinks a meal is something you bung in the microwave in the commercial break and crème brûlée is a wrinkle treatment. She's never expressed interest in nurturing a stick insect, let alone a baby.

And then…!

Anything can trigger it off. Someone at the office is pregnant; her friend from uni needs IVF… quite often it's her thirtieth birthday. Thirtieth birthdays are more stressful for the average woman than the Ides of March were for poor old Julius Caesar. Anyway, whatever does it she's a changed woman: unable to pass a Mothercare window, weeping over lambs in fields, sponsoring fifteen orphans in Botswana and painting the spare bedroom baby-blue with ducklings.

Now you know about babies; your sister has *three*. They leak at both ends, scream all the time and must have something in their mouth, even if it's only your Cup Final ticket.

Let a baby in your life and your youth is GONE.

Kaput.

Over.

You spend your time crawling round the floor looking for lost dummies and when you find them you have to lick all the fluff off before you can plug the baby's screams (but do it furtively because mothers become experts in the antisepsic department and spit has thirty-seven different forms of streptococci).

Later on they get cheeky, have to be taken to football practice or swimming lessons, or you have to get in a sack and make a prat of yourself on Sports Day because all the other imbecile fathers do.

And that's only if they're boys!

If they're girls it's ballet classes and nativity plays, which are pants unless your daughter is playing Mary and if she IS Mary you cry and have to pretend you're blowing your nose, which makes everyone turn round and look at you. And later still they have parties and trash the house and you have to turn up in the magistrates court when they're drunk and disorderly. And they get lost in the Sahara in their gap year and the worry makes you turn your toes up at forty-nine, which is way, way too soon.

'You can't buy babies but you sure as hell pay for them.'

Oh yes, you know about babies, and what you know says 'Don't do it'.

Useless to tell HER this. She has turned into a baby-making machine and you are the generator.

You try playing for time. 'Next year,' you say brightly. You promise her a month in Bermuda if she'll just hang on. She isn't listening. You point out that the flat isn't big enough for a baby and a 4.4 two-seater isn't a family car and who was scathing when Josh and Ria came to a party with a carrycot and doesn't she realize that a baby is the end of life as you both know it?

After this you have sex. Usually she leaps up and makes coffee. Tonight she lies still with her legs in the air 'just in case' and you realize she's stopped taking the pill. You sit on the bog all night wondering which god you've offended and promising never to drink again if he will render one or preferably both of you infertile. By the time she wakes up, you've taken a masterful pill and tell her it's condoms at dawn or nothing!

She appears to back off but actually gets sneaky. First of all it's the lacy-underwear ambush and then one day she brings home a baby which she is 'minding' for a friend. It's cute, alright, but you're relieved when its parents come to collect it and sure enough, he's hollow-eyed from lack of sleep and she smells mumsy.

> *'There is no greater commitment than*
> *the pram in the hall.'*

'See?' you say when they've gone. 'That's what it does to you. Is that what you want: to turn into a *Hausfrau*?'

She nods so violently you think her head'll come off then she bursts into tears, packs and calls a taxi. You offer to talk about it, but she says she doesn't talk to unfeeling monsters and that baby looked at you and held your finger and if you'd been a MAN you would have been MOVED!

To your surprise this makes you feel ashamed and, actually, it was quite a nice baby and its eyes did follow you around.

The taxi man is ringing the doorbell and she's crying and picking up her bags. You tell him to sod off and carry her to bed. As you do the deed, half of you is thinking that now you'll never get to climb K2 and the other half is thinking you must call him Alex after your dad and he'll be third generation at that school and when he gets a Nobel prize you'll be there, looking proud.

For a fleeting moment it occurs to you that it might be a girl and you won't know how to take her to the toilet – but then the mother-to-be nibbles your ear and you get really enthusiastic about things.

Boy or girl: *que sera sera.*

SHE SAYS... You've always wanted children. Sometime in the future. Between making MD and the menopause. After all, positively no one has babies early nowadays.

Well, no one *intelligent.*

Then one by one your girlfriends do it and they all give vivid descriptions of the birth process. Roughly

299

speaking, they fall into two groups: the ones who say it's like a bomb going off in your knickers and those who say it was a spiritual experience.

The first group are never going to have sex again.

The second are already checking ovulation dates.

They both ask you to be godmother because you're good at remembering birthdays.

'Once the toothpaste is out of the tube it's damn near impossible to get it back in again.'

For quite a while you find it amusing. When you do it (and you *will* do it) you'll do it *well*. Like anything else, it only requires forward planning and a little extra effort. You can be back at work by the fourth month and with a bit of luck the nanny will peel veg and do a bit of ironing.

As you watch your godchildren grow, you realize it's more than smocked rompers and talcum. They get red in the face and make little grunting noises when they're filling their nappy. They do this exactly three minutes after they've been changed, which is how you know they can tell the time.

If you bend down near their highchair they'll put lamb dinner in your hair.

You can't drink when you're breastfeeding and stretch marks never go away; they just turn silver and sinister, like water courses seen from outer space.

You have to wear dresses that button at the front so you can get your bosom out and if you do it in public some colonel from the shires calls the police.

You have to keep tissues in your pocket all the time and they're usually gummed up with snot or spew and you pull them out in front of the woman from the Conservative Association and have to pretend they're nothing to do with you and must have fallen from an aircraft.

The friend who once catalogued artefacts for the British Museum now watches *Teletubbies* and talks about nits and impetigo and when her little Johnny hits her in the face with a Hornby engine she just smiles. You realize she's turned into an android and any minute now her eyes will roll up and her works fall out of an opening in her stomach.

You remember that old saying about children: 'If you have none to make you laugh, you'll have none to make you cry'.

Those old soothsayers certainly knew what they were talking about.

'Love 'em or hate 'em, you're stuck with 'em.'

And then you miss a period! For four days you go to the loo on the hour just to check. You read up terminations in *The Family Book of Health* and decide you will if you have to – except you won't have to because you've always been careful.

You don't tell HIM until it's a week and then you see the phrase 'all the colour drained from his face' enacted before your eyes. When he's recovered, he says it's up to you and he'll stand by you whatever you decide. Then he goes off to sit cross-legged in the utility room and the sound of 'Om, Om' chanting fills the house.

You've always known he was highly strung but terror in a grown man is not a pretty sight.

When you've given him a stiff drink and rubbed his back, he asks you how it happened. Which really means 'How did *you let* it happen?'

He points out that one salary won't support the mortgage and you have a vivid mental picture of a man in Arab dress leading a donkey with a woman on it crossing her legs in the hope they make the inn in time.

Neither of you sleep that night. At four he goes to the all-night supermarket to get some booze, but somehow you feel guilty about drinking and phrases like 'foetal alcohol syndrome' come to mind.

Phrases you didn't even know you *knew*.

The next few days you loiter in arcades deliberately not looking at baby shops and you can feel your breasts swelling even though your conscious mind tells you this is an impossibility.

'Don't ask ME how it happened!'

On the tenth day you menstruate and have to hold on to the sink because you're weak with relief. You ring him on his mobile to give him the all-clear.

He doesn't say much except to ask why you're crying. He brings flowers when you come home and you sit either side of the kitchen tables knocking back gins as though it were a wake.

'So?' he says at last.

And you smile brightly and say, 'We can afford the patio now.'

And he says, 'S'pose so'.

Then you say 'We could try again' and you think he'll shake his head. Instead he says, 'I could do with an early night' – and that's when you realize you were born to have his children.

Deal with it

Babies should be approached with caution. They are a commitment besides which a marriage certificate pales into insignificance. That licence can be nullified with another piece of paper although it may cost you financially. A baby is *forever*. Nothing else is capable of providing as much entertainment, pride, worry or bafflement. Carefully considered, a baby is probably the best investment you will ever make – a friend for life. Entered into lightly, children can be a headache like no other, so think before you conceive.